Just Show Up

Also by Cal Ripken Jr.

The Only Way I Know

Play Baseball the Ripken Way

Parenting Young Athletes the Ripken Way

The Longest Season

Get in the Game: 8 Elements of Perseverance

That Make the Difference

Cal Ripken's Jr.'s All Star Series
for Young Readers

The Closer

Squeeze Play

Wild Pitch

Super Slugger

Hothead

The Longest Season

HARPER

NEW YORK . LONDON . TORONTO . SYDNEY

Just Show Up

And Other

Enduring Values

from Baseball's

Iron Man

Cal Ripken Jr

and James Dale

HARPER

A hardcover edition of this book was published in 2019 by HarperCollins Publishers.

JUST SHOW UP. Copyright © 2019 by CRJ, Inc. All rights reserved. Printed in the United States of America. No part of this book may be used or reproduced in any manner whatsoever without written permission except in the case of brief quotations embodied in critical articles and reviews. For information, address HarperCollins Publishers, 195 Broadway, New York, NY 10007.

HarperCollins books may be purchased for educational, business, or sales promotional use. For information, please email the Special Markets Department at SPsales@harpercollins.com.

FIRST HARPER PAPERBACKS EDITION PUBLISHED 2020.

DESIGNED BY WILLIAM RUOTO

Library of Congress Cataloging-in-Publication Data has been applied for.

ISBN 978-0-06-290675-5 (pbk.)

20 21 22 23 24   LSC   10 9 8 7 6 5 4 3 2 1

To my beautiful wife, Laura, who is always there for me
and has made me incredibly happy.
To my children, Rachel and Ryan, who have made me
proud and brought me joy since the day they were born.
To my "Bonus Kids," Madison and Trey: thank you for
letting me into your life.
You all always Show Up for me—thank you.

Contents

Contents

Introduction

I'm a ballplayer, from a baseball family. My father played, too; then he was a manager in the minor leagues, then in the majors. I was with one team—the Baltimore Orioles—for my entire career. I eventually broke Lou Gehrig's record for most consecutive games with my 2,131-game streak. I retired in 2001 and started Ripken Baseball, and we now have youth baseball facilities in Aberdeen, Maryland; Myrtle Beach, South Carolina; and Pigeon Forge, Tennessee; several others are in development. I've been a baseball broadcaster for the playoffs on TBS, and I've had the privilege of speaking to prominent organizations of Hollywood producers, Wall Street executives, union workers, and many others. I'm in the Hall of Fame—a great honor.

Introduction

The Orioles, 2,131 games, youth baseball, and the Hall of Fame: that's what most people know about me. So why write a book about enduring values? On the field and off, I've learned some basic principles of life, and today, they're still relevant, maybe more relevant than ever.

We live in challenging times. Bullying, name-calling, cutting corners, and sometimes just disregarding the truth have become accepted parts of all our lives. (I can almost hear my father, Cal Sr., saying, "You just don't do that.") The values and principles I grew up with aren't respected the way they used to be. I work with top leaders and spend days with kids at our youth baseball facilities, so I think I understand as well as anyone that there are some things that always make sense, some things that should last. It seems we could use some enduring values right now. I don't mean to tell other people how to live, but I do want to share what I've learned in case it's helpful.

I learned by listening to the wisdom of my father, but sometimes by ignoring his wisdom and having to learn the hard way. I learned from my mother, who was the ideal partner and the loving counterpoint to my father. I learned from winning the World Series, but I learned as much, if not more, from a long, painful losing season. I learned when to get mad at umpires and when not to.

Introduction

I learned from teammates and opponents who were role models and sometimes from guys who taught me what *not* to do. I learned from some good business decisions, some not so good ones, and a few lucky ones. I learned a lot from raising kids, from telling kids how life works, and then from listening to kids to really learn how life works. I learned from success and from failure. I'm still learning.

I believe in certain values and principles. And I try to live by them. Values matter, and I'm happy to share what's worked for me and what hasn't. That's what this book is about—not just baseball, but also life. It turns out they're a lot alike.

Chapter 1

Just
Show
Up

Just Show Up

Everyone has a 2,131

I played in 2,131 consecutive baseball games. That number broke Lou Gehrig's record, and eventually I went on to play in 2,632 straight games.

Everyone has a 2,131 of their own—just showing up. We each have personal streaks as a parent, as a friend, in business. Our job is to be there. The more reliable, consistent, and dependable you are, the better you're doing. Every day, every week, every year, someone is counting on you.

You raise children, you build a business, or you're there for your friends: if you just keep showing up, whether you set a record or not, you stand out—because people can count on you.

Just show up.

Why streaks matter

Streaks show that being there for your team, for other people—trying to win as a team—is more important than what might be good for you individually. If I could play and help my team, it would be selfish to take a day off. It's that simple. My streak was mostly considered a positive achievement. Occasionally it was criticized as a personal goal, but the people who criticized it missed the point. To me, showing up every day is a matter of principle. That's why I'm a fan of other people's streaks, in sports and in life.

Joe DiMaggio went on a fifty-six-game hitting streak in 1941. He got at least one hit in every game he played in from May 15 to July 16 of that season. If he hadn't been in the lineup for each one of those games—to have a chance to get a hit in each—there wouldn't have been a streak. More important, there wouldn't have been all those hits for his team. Joe showed up and did his job.

The University of Connecticut women's teams have had some of the greatest streaks in college basketball. They had a 111-game run heading into the 2017 NCAA Playoffs, aiming for a fifth consecutive national title. Even more amazing, when head coach Geno Auriemma took over in 1985, the team had had only *one winning season* in its entire history.

In 2017, UConn was upset in the Final Four by Mississippi State. All streaks end. But their meaning doesn't. The value of the achievement lasts. Then the chance to beat the old record is a challenge. That's something else I believe: whether in sports or business or life itself, tomorrow can be the start of another streak.

There are many other examples.

Senator Susan Collins, Republican from Maine, hasn't missed a single vote in Congress since she was first elected in 1996. She says she was elected to do her job, and to her that means doing it every day, every vote. *60 Minutes* has been running consecutively since 1968—from six weeks before Richard Nixon won the presidential election to today. *Saturday Night Live* has made people laugh since 1975. Bob Dylan has been on a tour nicknamed the Never Ending Tour since 1988; he averages about ninety concerts a year, and he's now in his late seventies. When asked why he played so many shows every year, he said, "These days, people are lucky to have a job. Any job. So critics might be uncomfortable with my working so much. Anybody with a trade can work as long as they want. A carpenter, an electrician. They don't necessarily need to retire."

One my other favorite streaks is the one belonging to Billy Joel. In January 2014, he signed on to play Madison Square Garden once a month for as long as his shows sold out. As of January 2019, he's played to almost sixty consecutive full houses at the Garden. When he was asked why he does it, Joel said, "I'm not doing it to break records. . . . I'm doing it because that's what I do." *Because that's what I do.*

That says it all. If you do your job, if you show up, you stand out. You might set records. Streaks can even keep you young. Nolan Ryan pitched for twenty-seven seasons, more than any other major-league player, and he struck out 5,714 batters, more than any other pitcher. He's also the all-time leader in no-hitters with seven, three more than his nearest competitor. Ryan could have stopped a season or two earlier and still held those records, but he didn't.

Reggie Jackson—a great player in his own right—said, "I saw Nolan Ryan throw 211 pitches in twelve innings one day. It messed him up so bad, he had to retire sixteen years later, when he was forty-six." Ryan said, "My job is to give my team a chance to win." And that was what he did.

Is the streak bigger than you?

There are those who might say that when you're trying to set a record, whether it's on a baseball field or in Congress or at a concert hall, you're doing it to make yourself look good, not for the good of the team or your colleagues or your profession. Some pretty respected people have felt that way—Joe Morgan, the great Cincinnati Reds second baseman, for example. There were times when Joe was critical of my streak. I never really knew why. Then, at an event called the Great Eight at the Yogi Berra Museum (for ballplayers who wore number 8, like Yogi, Joe, Willie Stargell, Carl Yastrzemski, and me), Joe came up to me and said, "I owe you an apology." He told me that when I was in the midst of the streak, he was mad at me, kind of disappointed. It was because when I first came up in the majors, Frank Robinson had said to Joe, "Look at Ripken—he's going to be the best that's ever played." Joe thought that meant that I'd hit a lot of home runs and make flashy plays, not that I'd play consistently, day after day. So Joe saw the streak as something that took away from my chance to do the "big stuff." But now, Joe was admitting he'd been wrong. I said, "Joe, I played the game because each day there's a challenge to try to win the game." I looked at it the way my dad looked at it, and that's my job today. My dad said, "You can't play tomorrow's game till it gets here. You can't replay yesterday's game. But this is today's challenge, and you should meet the challenge of today as best you can." To me, it was an honor to be able to do that and be counted on to do that, whatever happened, whatever my personal stats were, and wherever we finished.

A streak is not an end in itself. It's a way of doing things.

Wally Pipp

I wasn't born a person who was going to break the consecutive game record; I had to learn the importance of showing up, and one of the people who showed me that never even knew he would.

(I also had to learn the importance of always keeping some painkillers handy.)

Wally Pipp was a very fine baseball player. He had two years leading the home run category in the American League for the Yankees, who won three pennants in consecutive years in the early 1920s, as well as the World Series in 1923. Pipp was no slouch as a baseball player. Then one day in 1925, he got a headache and sat out a game. His place at first base was taken by a guy named Lou Gehrig. And baseball, not to mention Wally Pipp, was never the same again.

My dad often invoked the sad story of Wally Pipp. There were times in my early career when I would get in super late from a road trip—three, four, or five in the morning—and feel too tired to play the next game. This is natural in baseball; it might look like we're standing around a lot, but four or five hours on your feet, concentrating on every single play, can be draining. So sometimes I'd tell my dad that I was planning on skipping a game, but whenever I did so, my dad would simply tell me that if I gave someone else a chance to play in my position, he might get three hits, and I could be the Wally Pipp of my generation. It's fine to take a day off if you're ready to take a second day off and a third, or many, as

Wally Pipp had to. Or you can just be ready to play every day and not risk it.

I've used that story with my son, Ryan. He's a fine baseball player, but it takes commitment to keep going even when things are tough. I know I've told him about Wally Pipp, and I've told my wife's son, Trey, too.

Trey plays high-school lacrosse; he's a face-off guy, and a really good one. One day, he broke his stick during a face-off, and he had to go off the field to try to fix it. In the meantime, the backup face-off guy won three in a row, and it looked as though Trey wasn't going to make it back into the game. Afterward, I told Trey about Wally Pipp and suggested that he have a backup stick on hand—in fact, I told him he should have two or three. In sports you should be prepared to do whatever it takes to stay in the game. If you're trying to fix a stick when the guy on the field is playing great, you risk losing your spot for good.

Sometimes even bad streaks are good

The Orioles went on a losing streak in 1988. It lasted 21 games. What could possibly be good about losing that many games in a row? Well, adversity either destroys people and teams and families, or it brings them together as people, teams, and families. In '88, the entire sports world was following our games, but not in a good way. When we were 0–18, my brother Billy was on the cover of *Sports Illustrated*; the headline under his picture read, "The Agony of the Orioles." Fans came to the games and jeered more than cheered.

Off the field, however, the players bonded and propped each other up. We kept the pitchers from beating themselves up over another loss or a near-win that got away. The pitchers did the same for the rest of us, on the field and at bat. We had a shared experience, even if it wasn't a good one. When we finally won, in Chicago, we all breathed a sigh of relief, together, as a team. By the time we went into the next season, we couldn't have been a more tight-knit group, and we started winning. In fact, that season was the total opposite of the last one, piling up wins instead of losses. It inspired the fans' chants and signs: "Why not?" as in, why not this season? We played head-to-head with the Toronto Blue Jays to the very end, a three-game season finale, and only one year after our worst season, we finished a very close second.

One more thing came out of that losing season: a personal test for me.

The year 1986 had been Earl Weaver's last as Orioles manager. The team had had a rough season, finishing at the bottom of the AL East, 22$\frac{1}{2}$ games out of first place. In 1987, the O's were in bad need of new blood on the team and in the dugout. My dad, Cal Sr., who had been an Orioles coach, was named manager. We had another rough year, losing 95 games, because we were just beginning to make the moves to rebuild the team. But going 0–6 to start the '88 season, Dad was fired.

That really took the wind out of me. This was my father, probably the best role model and man I'd ever known. He was a proven coach and baseball man. It wasn't fair, by any measurement. He had inherited a team that needed major renovation from the bottom up. He knew what needed to be done—everyone did—and that it would take time; everyone knew that, too. Before anyone could begin to see results, he was let go.

The decision was made. Now, how would I react? The truth is, at first, not well. I was mad. I was hurt for him. I'm not good with things that aren't fair, and I'm worse with things that don't make sense. I thought what the front office did in firing him, and when they did it, were just plain stupid. I thought long and hard about whether I wanted to play someplace else. It was a close call.

The Orioles brought in Frank Robinson to manage, and Frank was as good a baseball guy as there is. I thought some more about what to do and finally decided the right thing was to show the world what we were made of, as a team and individually, each one of us, including me. Show up, do your job, and get out of this lousy streak, professionally and personally—that was the plan.

It wasn't easy, and it didn't fix the hurt. But I tried to find something good inside the bad. If this was a test, I was going to pass it. It was, after all, what my father had taught me. He wouldn't have quit. So I stayed, and I played, and we came back together as a team.

A streak shows character

Ernie Johnson Jr. is one of the premier sports broadcasters in America, covering baseball, golf, and basketball for Turner Broadcasting. Ernie, Ron Darling, and I were part of a broadcasting team for Major League Baseball on TBS. As a veteran broadcaster, Ernie was my mentor when I joined them on-air.

Back in 2003, Ernie was diagnosed with non-Hodgkin's

lymphoma, but he didn't tell anyone. He just went to his doctors, and they monitored the disease. Over the next three years, Ernie never missed a day or night of work. In 2006, it became clear he needed to undergo chemotherapy. Midway through the NBA season when he was on-air, he went public with his condition and announced his plan for treatment. But, Ernie being Ernie, he finished out the remainder of the season. In fact, he didn't miss broadcasting a game or event in baseball, golf, or basketball until June of 2006. By then, he was getting chemo regularly, losing his hair, feeling the fatigue and other side effects, and finally, under doctor's orders, he took some time off.

One year later, Ernie Johnson Jr. was back on the air.

The way he handled the challenge was remarkable, but maybe it shouldn't have come as a surprise. Ernie and his wife have six kids, four of whom are adopted, two from difficult backgrounds in Romania and Paraguay. One suffers with a crippling, life-threatening illness. Ernie and his wife take care of that child, who lives on a ventilator, at home, largely on their own. Ernie is just a man who never complains. He does what he does for his children. I guess Ernie had to break his work streak during chemo, but he never broke his character streak.

Just Show Up

Streaks are the long haul

Everything you do is a test of how well you do it, not just once or twice, but again and again, after your task has lost its newness or novelty, when it's just the daily repetition of what needs to be done. It doesn't matter what form it takes. Maybe it's just getting up every day and turning the lights on, doing business the way you're supposed to, and turning the lights off at night. Maybe it's being there for a friend when you're needed. Maybe it's being a consistent, reliable parent, one who's *there*, not just for your child's lead in the play, but also for the everyday stuff, like delivering a project to school because your child left it at home. Above all, it's not what you *mean* to do, it's what you actually do—actions, not intentions.

Ripken Baseball's business streak

People sometimes ask me what's made Ripken Baseball successful. The first thing I say is, let's not brag about success yet, but let's hope we're on our way. Our business model has changed and been refined over time. One thing has not changed, however. From day one, we set out to give kids—both boys and girls—a positive experience, and we've supported the experience with our four pillars: *Keep It Simple. Explain the Why. Celebrate the Individual. Have Fun.*

From Aberdeen to Myrtle Beach to Pigeon Forge, day in and day out, season after season, we've done what we said we'd do—provide a program that benefits kids above all. That means we don't say we've succeeded and we don't care about profit until and unless we deliver what young people and their parents are looking for. They're our customers. Without them, there's no company, no success. For us, it's *kids first, business second*. We try to bring together young athletes who want to learn skills and values with good coaches who can not only teach fundamentals but also instill positive attitudes. We create a program that is structured, sensitive to each child's needs. It builds individual skills but as part of the team performance. Naturally, some kids are better than others, but the team comes first. It's competitive in a healthy way—that's part of sports.

One thing is for sure. We're not here to be just another summer camp or a place to park kids while parents get away. We try very hard to deliver a positive, lasting experience for young athletes. That's not as common in youth sports as it could be. If there is one reason for our success, maybe that's it.

Friendship streaks

Because I've been in and around baseball as long as I can remember, it's not surprising that most of my friendships have come from the sport.

When I came up to the majors in 1981, I connected with Orioles first baseman Eddie Murray, who had arrived in Baltimore five years ahead of me. Eddie's not a guy prone to long speeches and life lectures—usually a word or two and setting a good example; he just quietly looked after me. We got closer and closer, with a kind of unspoken bond that became unbreakable over the seasons, and along the way we played on the World Series–winning team in 1983. Eddie was traded away later, but our friendship continued. I was happy to see him come back to the Orioles for one more year in 1996, and we've stayed close to this day. We might not speak for long periods of time, but that doesn't matter. The bond is there.

Then there's Brady Anderson, O's outfielder, whom I described at my Hall of Fame induction as "quite simply, my best friend." There's a lot packed into that short phrase. "Quite simply," meaning that's the bottom line, period. And "my best friend"—when I need to count on someone, I can count on Brady. Brady came to the team in 1988 and played there until 2001. (Speaking of streaks, for a long time he held the American League record of thirty-six games in a row with a stolen base.) I think I originally gravitated to him because he's just plain smart. He's a guy you can talk to about baseball, but we could also have conversations about history, philosophy, movies, and books. We came to count on each other in personal matters, too. We'd talk every day during the season, then not at all for the entire off-season, then pick it right up in spring training. After we both retired from playing, we realized that every day was the off-season, so it was up to us to keep up the friendship. It took more work, because we weren't in the dugout or locker room or on airplanes together—no 162-game schedule to automatically put us in contact. So we called regularly and managed to stay in touch. Now that he's VP of Baseball Operations with the Orioles, he's nearby again. We may not talk every single day, but I know he's there if I need him, and he knows the same. We have a friendship streak.

There's one friend who broke his own streak, and he did it for me.

Ernie Tyler was an umpire's attendant with the Orioles for over three decades—making sure all the umpires' needs were met, from meals to laundry to clean cleats to a full supply of "rubbed-up balls" (with Delaware River mud). Ernie hadn't missed a game in thirty-two years until my Hall of Fame day, in 2007. That day, he skipped work to come to Cooperstown to be there for me. That's a friend—pure Ernie. He was back on the job the next day.

Being an umpire's attendant might seem like a humble task, but if you looked at it the way Ernie did, you made sure you did it and did it right every game, every season. I wasn't alone in admiring the way Ernie did his job. Here was a guy in sports but in an unsung role, behind the scenes, whose obituary was featured in the *New York Times* with a humbling comparison of our two streaks. "From opening day in 1960 . . . Tyler was the umpire attendant for every Orioles home contest, a streak of 3,819 games. Then he skipped a game, but only one . . . to accompany [Ripken] to Cooperstown for his induction into the Baseball Hall of Fame."

That's a friendship and a streak, one that set a very

good example. His sons, Jimmy and Fred, went into "the family business" and have been working for the Orioles for over five decades in jobs similar to their father's.

Family streaks—no days off

There's a TV commercial in which a mom has a cold and wants to "call in sick," but as the announcer says, "Moms don't have a day off." Instead she takes Nyquil and Dayquil to keep on going. That's what parenting is—all day, every day. You can do it a thousand times, and do a thousand things right, but you don't get a free ride the next time you're up.

I once tried to count up how many times my kids had to go to the emergency room with a broken bone, or a gash, or a wound from stepping on a sea urchin, or whatever was the near-disaster that day. I lost count, and so did their mom. I remember holding my sixteen-month-old son in the ER so the doctor could stitch up his nose. I remember when he cracked his head open in a batting cage. I remember pulling a needle from that sea urchin out of his foot. Still, nobody says, "OK, you were there for twelve emergencies; you can take the next one off." Not only do you have to be there, but you have to say the right thing, make the right judgment, offer the right advice, listen well, weigh things, not get angry, and be wise— all in the face of challenges that never give you warning they're coming and for which you can never be prepared.

Can you make an error in parenting and make up for it by doing well for the rest of the day, the way you can in a baseball game? One of the most difficult things I ever dealt with was the issue of being there or not being there for my kids. My profession meant being out of town for half the season, 81 out of 162 games. In addition, there were spring training and personal appearances. But that problem wasn't unique to me—a lot of parents have jobs that keep them at the office late or take them out of town. When I was in town, during those 81 home games and during the off-season, I made sure I was there for the kids. I went to every school event or play or game I could. I grew up in a baseball family, and my dad was gone a lot, so I knew what it felt like. I did everything I could to be there for my kids. I drove them to school, I coached, I helped with homework, I took them to my "office," the ballpark. Did my home-streak make up for my away games? Did what I taught them stick when I wasn't there? I hope so. I didn't get everything right—far from it—but maybe what I did, and what their mother did, had something to do with the fact that they're good kids, or rather, good young adults. All you can do is show up and try your best.

Don't expect to be appreciated, though. That's not why you pursue a streak. That's not why you show up. You do it because it's what you do. It's your job.

Chapter 2

Success and Money Are Not the Same

Money is fine—there's no question that more is better than less. But I decided long ago, back when I didn't have much, that I wasn't going to let money be a measure of my happiness. I wasn't going to let money be an end in itself.

My dad was happy because he was lucky enough to

make a living—even if it wasn't a lot—in baseball his whole life. He didn't want to go to an office or knock on doors; he wanted to teach young guys how to make a squeeze play or field a two-hopper, to come home sweaty and do it all again the next day. (The story goes that when Cal Sr. signed his first contract with the Orioles, he didn't have a pen with him to sign it and had to borrow one from a fan.) Like my dad, I can honestly say I was happy in minor-league ball. Sure, I wanted to move up, but day-to-day I was doing what I wanted, playing baseball for a living, and that was all I wanted back then.

I think you should define your own success, on your terms, or else there will just never be enough money. If you do that, you can be "rich" in the most important way—your own happiness. I try to remind myself of what's important (and what's not), and mostly, I try to do what makes me happy. No one has the same definition of happiness, but it's crucial that you know what your definition is. I've been very fortunate to make a good living, but I got to do it by doing pretty much the same things in the majors that I did and loved in the minors—from the rookie league to single A, to AA, to AAA, to the O's. Playing baseball made me happy.

Success and Money Are Not the Same

Minor-league life lessons

I grew up around the minor leagues because my dad was a player, and then a coach in the minors for the first fourteen years of my life. Cal Sr. managed the Leesburg, Florida, Orioles in Class D the year after I was born; then he moved to Class B in the Fox River cities of Illinois, Indiana, and Iowa. Next he moved up to Class A, first to Aberdeen, South Dakota, and then with the Tri-City Atoms in Kennewick, Washington, and next on to the Miami Marlins. From there he went to Class AA with the New York Pioneers, to Rochester in AAA, to the Dallas–Fort Worth Texas Spurs, and then to the Orioles of Asheville, North Carolina. And my dad worked two or three jobs in the off-season, too. I remember when a lot of kids had these expensive athletic shoes, my mom found a place where she got us three pairs of shoes for $2.99. My dad's success wasn't measured in money. It was doing what you wanted to do and hopefully moving up to the next level.

The same went for me as a player in the minor leagues. You weren't there to make a lot of money; you were there to get to the majors. In the minors, if we wanted a raise, we "negotiated" by writing a letter to the farm director (and usually got turned down). A big raise might be $200 more a month, but it wasn't about whether we made $800 a month or $1000. No matter what we got, we didn't have enough to live very well. In Miami, we rented furniture, but we didn't have enough for a television, so instead we played a lot of cards, sitting on that rented furniture. All-you-can-eat buffets were like gourmet dinners for us; we ate all we could, for sure.

There was a reason for all this. We were there to perfect our baseball skills and make it to the majors. It was our grad school. The fact that we got paid at all was a plus, and the teams knew it. Our bargaining power, on a scale of one to ten, was zero. Even so, we wouldn't have traded our jobs to be anywhere else (except the major leagues, of course).

An agent who served tuna sandwiches

When major-league teams start to get serious with you, slick sports agents start coming around to take you out for a steak dinner. They're well dressed, drive fancy cars, and take you to a restaurant with reservations and real tablecloths. It's not subtle, but who doesn't go for a big steak, a baked potato, and a few beers?

Success and Money Are Not the Same

Nevertheless, the agent who impressed me the most didn't buy me a steak dinner. Instead, he set up a meeting at his modest office in a nearby, not very fancy building. We sat around his conference table with tuna sandwiches he'd brought in from a deli. (In fairness, I think I had a choice of tuna or egg salad.) The agent, Ron Shapiro, had represented Orioles third baseman Brooks Robinson and, at that time, eight or ten more Orioles. He started the meeting by saying, "Cal, don't hire me to get you the richest rookie contract in history. I'm here to work with you to make sure you have a long career, so that at the end of it, you can continue to live well, have a family, and achieve your goals." No hype. No sizzle. Just substance.

Sold.

Ron's approach wasn't for everyone, but it was right for me. I stayed with the Orioles for my whole career, and I stayed with Ron my whole time with the O's. How did I know at such a young age what mattered and what didn't? Maybe I was lucky. Maybe it was growing up in baseball. Maybe it was my dad and his values. I like to think I'd grown up with some grounding in reality. Substance, no sizzle.

Maybe I just liked tuna fish.

The bottom is a good place to start

There's a minor league for everything.

One of the best lessons in the value of starting at the bottom came from my agent's son, Mark Shapiro. Like his dad, Mark wanted to go into sports, but he was drawn to the management side. A few years after he graduated from college, he wrote letters to every major-league team's front office. He didn't take advantage of his father's clout for introductions. He just wrote cold-call letters, and he got turned down by every team except one, the Cleveland Indians. What got them interested in him was the offer he made in his letter that he would "do anything at all," even run errands or get coffee. The Indians took him up on his offer, put him at a desk in the middle of a hallway, and had him do the most menial tasks, picking up players at the airport, poring over their stats, studying up-and-comers, scouting opposing teams, and making sure the coffee machines were full.

Mark didn't see the work as beneath him or menial. He saw it as his internship, his minor-league break, and he took every opportunity to show his dedication. He did everything they asked and more, getting in early, staying late, and always volunteering. Eventually, he got promoted to a real desk in a real office, and he was moved up again, and again, and again, until one day Mark Shapiro became one of the youngest general managers in the game, leading the Indians' total rebuilding. Later, he was wooed away to become president of the Toronto Blue Jays. His version of the minors—starting at the bottom—took him to the top of the majors.

Free agency isn't always free

After six years in the major leagues, if you haven't signed a contract for the following season, you can file for free agency, meaning you can accept outside arbitration or shop yourself to another team. It's an important right, and one that was hard-won by the Players Association. But freedom is a double-edged sword. If you do accept arbitration and win a bigger salary, your current team has to pay you more than they would have, and you may have created an adversarial relationship with the team. If you lose and don't get an increase, there might be hard feelings between you and your club.

Free agency means you *can* leave, but it may also mean you *will* leave. In other words, once you shop the market, your current team could decide they can't afford you and don't want to try to match another offer. Then you're stuck moving to a higher-paying team that you might not want to play for in a city you don't want to live in.

I decided early on that I wanted to live in Maryland and play for the Orioles, if possible, for my whole career. Was I hurting my negotiating power? Was I leaving money on the table? Maybe, maybe not. However, I had communicated that as a dedicated player, I was part of the worth of the franchise, an asset for the team's fan base. That, in itself, had a value to the team. And even though my first choice was to stay, I could still leave, when and if my contract expired.

In fact, I once got pretty close to going. After the 1987 season, the Orioles and I were trying to do a multiyear deal, but we couldn't seem to get it done. About ten minutes before the midnight deadline for free agency, we inked a one-year deal that got me what I wanted for the time being. I could stay with the O's and retain my free agency option for the following year. As a result, when my father was fired after six games in 1988, I was eligible to be a free agent at the end of the year. Because of the way he was treated, I wasn't feeling too good about my relationship to the team, and I made no secret of my feelings. Just the possibility that I might file for free agency was enough leverage to help me get a good deal. In August 1988, I signed for three years with an option to extend. That taught me a valuable lesson: sometimes your leverage doesn't have to be stated. Just the idea that it's possible to exercise it may carry more power than actually using it.

One of the many things that matters more than money: control

Here's another lesson I learned over and over: making a lot of money doesn't mean you get to determine your own destiny. That isn't true just in sports. Ask the CEO of a public company, who has to answer to analysts and shareholders or the rock star who has to hide from fans when she goes out for Starbucks.

I never set out to make headlines or break the bank as the highest-paid player in the game or the guy who got the biggest bonus. Control was always more important to me. Playing where I wanted to play, a no-trade clause, even having the right to play basketball in my free time—these things mattered more than mere dollars. Control is especially important in the big leagues, where your life could change any day with a trade, an injury, or another player coming along to take your spot. You can't control everything, but you can have some say-so. That's not something money can buy.

I wanted to play close to my hometown and come home to my house after a home game. This was far better than the threat of waking up one day and finding out I'd been traded across the country to join a team that I didn't want to play for. Longer-term stability and security—even if it meant passing up what might have been more money—and influence on what position I played mattered way more than being the highest-paid shortstop, though I also didn't want to give up fair market value for any of these things. Of course, a lot of this stuff is up to the manager and the club, but I wanted a voice. I was very happy to take a good, respectable paycheck in return for getting as much control as possible over my life.

Respect is worth something, too

Edward Bennett Williams, Orioles owner and a famous trial attorney, was an enormously successful, larger-than-life guy, and he could be very intimidating. In the off-season, the team would ask us to make appearances. I did as many as I could fit in, but at the end of the 1983 season, after we'd won the World Series, I was physically and mentally beat, and I desperately needed to get enough rest to be ready for spring training.

The Orioles publicity department asked me to go down to the Jefferson Hotel in Washington, DC, for an event, and I just felt I was too wiped out and had to decline. The next day, I got a call from EBW. The first thing that impressed me was that he called me directly—no assistant or secretary getting me on the line and saying, "I'll put Mr. Williams on." Just EBW saying, "Cal, I know that you've gone above and beyond what anyone could expect in promoting the Orioles this off-season, and I understand why you declined our event, but I would look at it as a personal favor to me if you would reconsider. This event is very important to me."

It became an easy yes. Of course, he was the owner, but he'd also called me personally.

When I arrived at the event, Mr. Williams came right over, welcomed me, and introduced me to everyone. He thanked me for changing my plans and for making the extra effort to be there. Edward Bennett Williams was probably the most important guy in the room, and I was still a young kid hoping to make it in the big leagues, but he treated me with dignity. There was a simple reason why he behaved the way he did; he believed that if you respect people, you treat them correctly.

I never forgot that, and I've tried to follow his example. Respect is everything.

Good contracts are good for both sides

In 1992, on my thirty-second birthday, after playing in 1,698 consecutive games, and after almost a year of negotiations, Ron Shapiro made a deal with Orioles president Larry Lucchino for $30.5 million over five years ($32.5 with a post-retirement front-office role). It was reported by the *New York Times* to be the biggest contract in baseball, edging out Bobby Bonilla's $29 million deal with the New York Mets. But in case we need more proof that money is not a measurement of success—at least not for long—in the same *Times* article, it was reported that in the upcoming year, Ryne Sandberg's deal with the Chicago Cubs would be extended from four to five years and at $31.8 million would be bigger than mine. Then Barry Bonds passed Sandberg, and on and on.

Nevertheless, I was happy. My contract gave me peace of mind, and I needed that. There were no more what-ifs. I wouldn't be thinking about where I'd be for the next five years. I wouldn't be preoccupied with free agency. I wouldn't be feeling that I had a contract expiring. I wouldn't be shopping for, or even thinking about, another team. I wouldn't worry that if I had an off-week or month or even season, anything would change. It meant I'd probably play my entire career with one team, the Baltimore Orioles.

My last contracts with the Orioles— good for me, good for them

Eventually, though, those five years were up, and I negotiated my next three contracts myself.

Ron Shapiro had had a falling out with Orioles owner Peter Angelos over negotiations for another of Shapiro's clients, Orioles broadcaster Jon Miller. Because I got along well with Peter, both Ron and I felt it was best for me to meet with the owner one-on-one; Ron and I could still get together to discuss strategy. Peter Angelos made his fortune winning huge asbestos settlements from some of the largest companies in the world, and he has a reputation as an aggressive lawyer and tough negotiator. I found that to be the case. He doesn't give in on a deal easily.

Peter is also fair, however. He recognized the two main things that he and the team wanted from me: one, to continue to play well and produce, and two, to help with attendance. I'd played well over my whole career—the streak got a lot of attention—and it looked as though I had a good shot at the Hall of Fame. He also knew that I wanted two main things: one, to be at home (i.e., in Baltimore); and two, to be paid fairly by the standards of the game at the time. At that stage of my career, I didn't feel that I had anything to prove, and I didn't want to think about playing for another team. Mostly I wanted to finish my career where I'd started it and to do so with a good, fair contract in hand, even if it meant leaving some money on the table.

I enjoyed negotiating with Peter. I found him to be candid and straightforward, smart and strategic, fair and reasonable. One thing you could count on was that when he said we had a deal, we had a deal—his word and his handshake were as good as any contract. After two years of dealing directly with him, by the time of my final contract, our meetings were brief. Peter just said, "How about the same as last year?" and I agreed. We'd shake hands, and a couple days later his office sent over the contract, just the way we'd agreed to it. He knew there was more to me than money. And I knew he respected me.

Somebody always has more money than you

No matter how much you make, somebody will make more. Today's record-breaking salaries and bonuses will be history before you blink. In 1930, during the Depression, when Babe Ruth wanted $80,000 and a reporter supposedly told Ruth that President Herbert Hoover only made $75,000, Ruth replied, "I know, but I had a better year than Hoover." In 1980, when Nolan Ryan broke the million-dollar barrier, everybody was sure that was the most you could pay a grown-up for playing kids' games. In 1997, Albert Belle got $10 million, ten times what Ryan made. Then Alex Rodriguez signed a record-setting ten-year deal worth $275 million, only to be beaten by Giancarlo Stanton's thirteen-year $325 million contract.

Today those deals are hardly at the top of pro sports. In 2016, NFL quarterback Cam Newton made over $53 million; NBA star LeBron James made $77 million; and Cristiano Ronaldo, soccer player for Real Madrid, totaled $88 million. Then LeBron signed a deal in 2018 with the Lakers for $154 million! In Hollywood, lots of stars make over $100 million from one movie. Businesspeople like Bill Gates of Microsoft, investor Warren Buffett, Jeff Bezos of Amazon, and Mark Zuckerberg of Facebook are multi-billionaires. But their records will all be broken. After all, Zuckerberg wasn't even on the billionaire list until 2008.

Are some people overpaid? Sure. In the end, though, no one is paid more than the business they're in can afford, at least not for long. At a dinner party in DC, I heard Jack Kemp, former Buffalo Bills quarterback and later a US senator, say that his own son, a young pro quarterback, was overpaid. Jack himself never made more than $15,500 in the NFL. He was picked up for $1,200 by the AFL Bills and finally, when he became a star, was paid better, at least for those times, but almost nothing by today's standards. His son was being paid $300,000 to be a backup quarterback, and Jack said, "How can they pay him that much to sit on the bench and wait for the other guy to get hurt?"

I disagreed with Jack and said so. "Your son is one of

maybe fifty to sixty players good enough to play pro quarterback. If the starter goes down, the whole game rides on your kid. The game could mean the division championship, the conference, maybe the chance to get to the Super Bowl. Today, the game is big business, bigger than ever. That's what happens in sports. The dollars keep going up. The owners make more, and the players should make more, too. And plenty of backups have gone on to be stars. He's worth that and more." To me, you should get what you're worth, but you still shouldn't judge your life by it.

Money is no measure of real accomplishment or happiness. I made more than my dad or the guys in his era, and whoever came after me made more than I did. If you measure your life in money, you'll always come up short.

Youth baseball may not be the next Google or Uber

When I started thinking ahead to retiring from playing pro ball, I had to think carefully about what I wanted to do with my post-baseball life. One of the options was to be a spokesperson for a company, maybe capitalize on my name and records. I would probably have been paid well for it, too, and even today, I still do speaking engagements and endorsements, but it's not my full-time career.

I wanted more. I wanted to pass along the lessons I'd learned in sports to young kids—girls and boys—the same lessons I tried to pass along to my own daughter and son. So my brother Bill and I started a business devoted to youth sports. Is it a way to get rich? I don't know; that's not why we did it. You'll probably never see us on Shark Tank or in the Forbes 400, but the job is something I know and understand, and more important, it's something that needs to be done.

The lessons we aim to instill are simple but timeless: to play fair, to play as a team, to win with grace and lose the same way, and most of all, to do what you like doing, not what someone else tells you to like doing. If, along the way, we help some kids go on to play at the next level and the next, then that's great—but many won't. However, we hope all of them will learn the lessons and take them with them through life.

We don't want kids to come to Ripken Baseball because a parent or a coach told them to, to impress a girl or a boy, or to put something on a college application. If a young person would rather stay indoors and make You-

Tube videos or build model airplanes, then that's great. Kids should do what makes them happy. We hope kids come to us because they love baseball, want to get better at it, and want to be around other kids and coaches who love the game. There's no guarantee anyone is going to have a career in baseball. Do it because you love it.

I know that principle well. I grew up in a family that never had much in the way of luxuries. We didn't have fancy cars in the driveway. We had one TV, and it didn't work so well all the time. My dad wanted to be a major-league player, but he didn't make it that far. Instead, he stuck with the game as a scout, coach, and manager. It was what he loved, so he was happy, and we were happy. Money, or the money we didn't have, just didn't matter. Doing what you love and doing it well matters more. That was the family lesson.

My kids' real inheritance

When you die, what will you leave your children? Your house, your car, your life savings? Or what you stood for? I hope what my kids get is a collection of values from me and from their mom.

My son is trying to be a major-league ballplayer. So far, he's played high-school ball in Baltimore; college ball at South Carolina and at Indian River State Junior College; and then in the minor leagues for the Auburn (New York) Doubledays, an affiliate of the Washington Nationals, and for the Aberdeen Ironbirds and DelMarva Shorebirds, both Orioles affiliates in Maryland. He's a first baseman, and he's been at it since 2014. Will he make it to the big leagues? It's hard to say. He's good, but is he good enough? Some days he asks me if he should keep at it. My answer is, "Do you want to?" If it's what he wants, he should keep going. Nothing I or his mom—or a coach or a sportswriter looking for copy—says matters.

My daughter is in sports, too, but in a very different role. She's the Director of Community Outreach in the University of Colorado Athletic Department, working with local organizations, arranging programs with CU athletes and facilities, and building bridges between the community and the school. She tells me she finds it very rewarding. It's clearly not a way to make a fortune, but she loves Colorado, she loves sports, and she loves working with young people.

I like to think I've given my kids some good things and some values, but I also know I gave them something that can at times be perceived as a negative: the name Ripken. For my son, Ryan, it can be particularly tough; it's not as though there are tons of Ripkens in baseball, and it's natural, if unfair, to compare him to me.

The name is also tough for my daughter, Rachel. When she was younger, she worked a summer job for Ripken Baseball, and she took it very seriously, partly because that's who she is but also because she's rightly very sensitive about her last name. I wasn't there every day, so it wasn't as if she were trying to impress Dad. Still, she did everything asked of her and a lot more, working long hours doing the most menial tasks, like washing out Gatorade coolers. I lost track of how many people pulled me aside to tell me she was the hardest worker they'd had all summer. Rachel knew she had to prove her worth beyond her name, and she did so.

I'm told she has the same work ethic out in Boulder, in her outreach work for CU sports. She is very hands-on; she works weekends and late into the evenings. This doesn't happen because I told her to—but because she knows that she has one shot to prove her worth. I can't change their names from Ripken, but no matter: she and Ryan are making their way despite the name (and, I hope, a little bit because of it and the values it represents).

Just Show Up

My kids are fortunate. They can do what makes them happy because they have the safety net of successful parents. But I hope they would do it anyway. I hope they'd follow the example of their parents, their grandparents, and other role models around them. I hope their real inheritance is doing what makes them happy.

Chapter 3

Play Fair—Win Fair

When I was a kid, I loved to win, so much so that I would even bend the rules a bit to ensure a victory. I even cheated at the card game canasta against my grandmother, who was losing her eyesight. Because she couldn't see well, I could draw more cards from the deck than I was supposed to on my turn, but instead of feeling good, the victory felt sort of empty.

Somewhere along the line, I realized that all I was proving to myself was that I was good at cheating. I wanted to be good at playing the games. Playing fairly, within the rules, I could find out if I was really good. So instead of breaking the rules, the rules became my best friends.

Now, I didn't come to this epiphany all by myself. It might make a really nice story, but it wouldn't be true. The truth is, my parents were rule followers. In our house, there was always a right way (and a wrong way) of doing things, even down to board games, which we played a lot. We were constantly looking up the rules on the inside of the box lid to make sure we were playing the game right. I can still conjure up a mental picture of my dad looking up the official rules of Major League Baseball, just like checking out whether you *have* to charge rent when someone lands on your property in Monopoly. Knowing the rules so you could win by the rules was important.

My father, Cal Sr., played by the rules, practiced the rules, and instilled the rules in me and my brothers and all the players he coached. To him, playing fair wasn't an option or choice; it was what you did, plain and simple. He didn't give us lectures, but he constantly reminded us, "If it's worth doing, it's worth doing right." He lived that way, so we did, too. If he saw me or my brothers doing something that wasn't right—say, trying to take a shortcut in our chores—he would point it out: "Cal, you just don't do that." There was no long discussion; there were no loopholes or excuses. "You just don't do that." My mom was the same. We never questioned it because it just was the way things worked. Maybe some people can look the other way when they or their kids do something wrong, especially if it's "just this once" or "to win the game." Not Cal Sr. or Vi Ripken. Every time we did a job or chore, my mom or dad would inspect it, and when we did it the right way, they'd say so: "Nice job. You should feel good about it."

Many years earlier, the phrase "the Oriole way" had become the embodiment of the team's attitude and behavior, and that way of doing things extended to our house. It was the way we lived at home—"The Ripken way"—and I still practice it, and we try to pass it on at Ripken Baseball today.

Why play fair, by the rules? Playing fair doesn't guarantee winning. Should you do it because other people tell you to? Maybe, but other people's values aren't necessarily yours. Should you do it because you're setting a good example? Sure, that's a good by-product of playing fair, but it's not the only reason. I play fair—by the rules—because it's important to *me*. When I look in the mirror, I can feel good about what I've done. It means that when you win, you'll know it was the best win you could have;

you've earned it. There can be no footnotes or asterisks next to those wins. The more you develop a respect for the rules, and the more you compete, the more your sense of fairness evolves. No set of rules can cover everything, however, and it's in the gray areas where your own values have to come into play.

You can play by the rules and still not play fair

In baseball (and other games) you can play by the official rules and, to me, still not be playing fair. Take the hidden-ball trick. It's probably been around since the invention of the game. There are lots of variations, but here's one way it works: Say a batter hits the ball deep to left field. He takes off, rounds first, and heads for second as the left fielder throws the ball to the second baseman. The second baseman catches it, but not before the batter has completed a stand-up double. Now, instead of tossing the ball back to the pitcher for the next batter, the second baseman *pretends* to throw it back but instead hides it in his glove. The pitcher *pretends* to catch it. The pitcher stands behind the rubber, rubbing the imaginary ball, giving the runner a false sense of security that he can take a lead off the bag. At that point, as soon as the runner steps off the base, the second baseman tags him out.

The hidden-ball trick can be done at any base, and it's perfectly legal according to the rules of Major League Baseball. But I don't like it. I don't like the idea that it's hidden or that it's a trick. I don't like the idea of acting out a make-believe skit to fool the opponent. It's not fair by my rules. My dad always told me there was no place in professional baseball for the hidden-ball trick, so that's that. Some of my old teammates would disagree, but to me, it wasn't part of the game. One time one of my teammates was working the trick and gave me the "shush" sign to keep it to myself. Instead, I walked right up to the runner and said, "The second baseman has the ball. Stay on the bag." I don't know if the runner believed me or thought it was another part of the trick.

Not only is it bush league to me, but also it works only once, and then you get a reputation for being the guy not to trust. That's not how I want to be looked at; I don't want to be the guy who fools the other guy. I want to beat him, but I don't want to do it by fooling him. By not doing the trick, I found I developed trust and respect from my opponents. Sometimes, I've even gotten helpful information from the other team, maybe because they could trust me.

What about stealing signs? Most people in baseball think it's OK for a base runner to relay the catcher's signs to the hitter. It's considered OK by the rules, not because the rules say it's legal, but because the rules don't address it. It's definitely *not* OK by my rules, for a lot of reasons. My basic disagreement is that it fundamentally changes the spirit of competition, because instead of it being a fair battle of batter versus pitcher, it gives the batter an unfair edge, In my rules, the pitcher and batter are in a duel. Whatever one can learn from the other is fine, but interceding to help one of them is not fine.

A couple of years ago, I was in New York on business with my team. We finished our meetings early, and my CEO at Ripken Baseball suggested we stop by and meet Aryeh Bourkoff, the founder of the investment banking firm Lion Tree. Aryeh had grown up in Baltimore. I hadn't known that, but I found out almost the moment I walked in. Aryeh opened his desk drawer, pulled out an old photograph of the two of us from when he was ten years old, and told me the story behind it.

The Orioles used to put together a traveling basketball team made up of our players, and we were sent out to play against faculty, alums, or players they'd recruit at local high schools, clubs, and organizations as part of a community-relations tour. Sometimes we'd mostly entertain, as in a Harlem Globetrotters exhibition, but sometimes the games were highly competitive. The Orioles and the school would publicize the event, and pretty large crowds would show. It was a good way to build a bond with our hometown fans, an opportunity to sign autographs and create grassroots support for the team. Most of the fans were polite, but sometimes it could get a little crazy when we would sign autographs. It turned out that Aryeh was at one of those games, but being a little guy of ten, maybe four and half feet tall, he practically got run over by bigger fans. After I'd signed a bunch of autographs, I was backing my way off the floor for the second half, trying to escape. Almost out the door, I heard a voice say, "Could you just let him take a picture with you?" It was Aryeh's mother, not shoving, not pushing, not waving a pen at me, just asking nicely. I looked down and found this little guy, and I knelt next to him while his mother snapped a picture. Aryeh was forty years old as he told me the story, but he said he'd kept that photo with him ever since he was a kid. He said it reminded him about doing the right thing, just because it's right.

When I met him in New York, he was busy building his digital media business, and he thought of possibly working with me in creating content for platforms like YouTube or podcasts, programs for parents and kids on the values of hard work, perseverance, and fair play. Whenever he tells the story of the photo with me, it connects with people. Who knows where it will lead, but I like to think that it shows that fairness can have nice rewards, even if they come thirty-some years later.

Sometimes you play fair a long time before you win (and you don't know for sure *that* you *will* win)

Today my company has baseball complexes, called the Ripken Experience, in Aberdeen, Maryland; Myrtle Beach, South Carolina; and Pigeon Forge, Tennessee, with some others on the drawing board. The facilities have multiple fields, regulation-size diamonds, and youth diamonds, each named after historic ballparks and each with state-of-the-art synthetic playing surfaces, training rooms, pitching mounds, batting cages, practice fields, two-day, three-day, and weeklong tournaments, plus hotel and recreation, everything to make the visit great for the kids in the program and for everyone in a family. They're all based on the ideals we believe in, practice, and teach.

Is that how all this "playing fair" stuff paid off? Well, not right away. Let me explain how we got here.

In 1995, the Major League Baseball Players Association Union got together and gave me a $75,000 gift, in honor of my breaking the consecutive-game record, to help me build a youth field in my hometown, a "field of dreams." I was humbled by that gift, but when I tried to spend it, I realized you can't build a lot of dreams on $75,000. I started thinking about how we could leverage the seed money to build something bigger, maybe four fields, a real complex, a place where my brother Billy and I could bring back some of the lessons my dad had taught in his baseball school.

Like most things in life, it was a lot easier said than done. First we pursued a deal to acquire independent (non-MLB-affiliated) minor-league teams, but that didn't work out. Then we were asked to bid on USA Baseball's possible move to Aberdeen. We pitched hard, developed great ideas, shared them openly, but lost out to another bidder. Then we had a chance for the contract to build the complex for USA Baseball at their new home in

Durham, North Carolina—more good ideas shared but another setback and more disappointment. After that, once we were finally getting our footing with our Aberdeen complex, we were given the opportunity to partner with the key folks at the summer resort of Myrtle Beach, South Carolina. And we won! Myrtle Beach became the first Ripken complex beyond Aberdeen, and the prototype for an entire business model. We had lost a lot of things along the way—our first minor-league partner, the USA Baseball headquarters, a USA Baseball design competition, and a lot of good of ideas, too. But we played fair throughout, and in the end we won. We won by learning, by refining our ideas, by making Aberdeen better, and then Myrtle Beach, and then Pigeon Forge, and hopefully every complex we build in the future. Does it always work that way? Of course not—but when it does, it feels great.

Nobody fools anybody in a good baseball trade

A lot of people in baseball think the only good trade is one in which you get a good ballplayer and pawn a worse player off on the other team. If you must trade a good player to get a good player, the common wisdom is that you don't make that trade in your own division. The Red Sox don't want to make the Yankees stronger and then play the Yankees, for instance.

I disagree. I think that's not only not fair; it's dumb. I learned the way the Orioles always did it, from before the time I played until well after. I say the best trades happen when both sides get someone they want and need. If we had a first baseman with promise, who wasn't going to play much with us because we had a Hall of Famer like Eddie Murray already in that position, it would be best for us to trade the promising guy for another good guy we need, say an outfielder or relief pitcher. This would potentially make both teams stronger. When there's relative parity in a trade, a number of things accrue. The two teams tend to trust each other and might want to make further deals, and the games between the teams then come down to how well each club plays, not just one player or another. On the flip side, stick the other team with a loser, and they'll never want to make another deal with you, or they'll be waiting for the time they can stick you with a stiff. It's the hidden-ball trick of baseball trading; it's not fair, and in fact, it's kinda dumb.

Trades good for both sides are not only the Orioles'

way. Ask Mark Shapiro. When he ran the Cleveland Indians, he always believed in trades that were good for both
sides. (He grew up a Baltimore fan, so maybe the Oriole
way rubbed off on him.) "Your goal in doing trades is to
have them be a win-win," Shapiro says. He engineered
the controversial trade, halfway through the 2002 season, of two Cleveland pitchers, minor-league player of the
year Tim Lee and All Star Bartolo Colón. They went to
the Montreal Expos in exchange for some relatively un-
known prospects and first baseman Lee Stevens. Among
the unknowns were pitcher Cliff Lee, who went on to
average 15 wins a season for the next three years and win
the Cy Young award in 2008; center fielder Grady Size-
more, who became the Indians' leadoff batter and an All
Star averaging 25 home runs and 78 RBIs; and Brandon
Phillips, who didn't get much of a chance in Cleveland
but went to the Reds, where he averaged 21 homers and
81 RBIs. Proof that it was a win-win was Colón's finishing the season with 20 wins and later being named a Cy
Young winner. Shapiro explains it this way: "You want
the player you send to the other team to provide them
with what they want. You're not looking to steal players
and win trades. You like trades to be a foundation for a
future trade." Shapiro moved to the Toronto Blue Jays,

practicing the same philosophy. Then the Blue Jays faced his former team, the Indians, in the 2016 baseball playoffs. The Indians won the American League pennant, not because they'd gotten the better of other clubs in trades but because their total team—all players, all coaches—beat another very good total team.

That's fair.

But everybody does it (cheating, that is)

Everybody drives over the speed limit.

Everybody cheats a little on income taxes.

Everybody tells "little white lies."

Everybody says the traffic was bad when they're late.

Everybody tastes the grapes in the grocery store before buying them.

Lots of people "forget" to count all their shots on the golf course.

Lots of people promise to call you back and then don't.

Lots of people find wallets and don't return them.

Lots of people cut in lines.

Some people park in loading zones.

Some people bump your car and don't leave a note.

Some people steal towels from hotels.

Some people rob banks.

Where's the line between what everybody does and what no one should do? Is "everybody does it" just an excuse for doing the wrong thing? I'm not perfect. I do some of these things, but I do try to do the right thing. There are no fairness police—just ourselves and our sense of what's right and wrong.

When I was a kid, my dad didn't do the grocery shopping often, but when he did, sometimes I'd go with him and sit up in the little seat in the cart. First thing he did was go down the candy aisle and grab a box of chocolate-covered peanuts; we ate them while shopping. By the time we'd finished, we'd have eaten the whole box. I thought, uh-oh, this is wrong. Then, at the checkout, he'd show the empty box to the cashier so she or he could add it to the bill. He was his own fairness cop.

Corking bats, pine tar, spitters, and thumbtacks

Until a few years ago, some batters were known to "cork" their bats—bore out the core of the bat and fill it with cork. Supposedly, corking had a "trampoline effect," so the batter could swing faster, and the ball would go farther. Later, MythBusters, the Discovery Channel television show, proved that corked bats are somewhat lighter but actually transfer less force to the ball, so they don't really do anything.

The use of pine tar was also popular, first on the handle to get a surer grip on the bat, which was perfectly legal, but later on the barrel of the bat, which was not. Some people believed it would not only give you a better grip but would make for better contact with the ball. No one ever proved pine tar worked, either for grip or contact.

Then there are spitters. Pitchers have been using the spitball for decades, and it can work. If you get enough slippery substance on the ball, it shoots out of the pitcher's hand without the same spin as a regular pitch, so it drops like a sinker—making it harder to hit. At one time, spitters were legal, or at least tolerated. But since then, the game cracked down on them and enforced the rules. Then the challenge became finding ways to get away with the spitter. The definition of a spitter has come to include a pitch with almost any substance to make the ball slippery. Yankee pitcher Whitey Ford created what he called a "gunk" by combing a weird bunch of things—baby oil, resin, and turpentine—and then applying it to the baseball from an old underarm deodorant dispenser. There is some evidence that Yogi Berra once used Ford's concoction on his armpits, thinking it was actual deodorant. Another favorite lubricant is hair gel. Gaylord Perry wrote a book called *Me and the Spitter*, in which he fessed up to his techniques: hiding Vaseline on his hat brim or in his glove or having dry soap on his pants that he could rub with his sweaty palms to make a slippery coating. Should Perry and Ford get credit for being creative by using any weapon they could get away with? The answer, to me, is simple: Spitballs can give the pitcher an unfair edge over the hitter. Unfair, whether it's creative or not, is still unfair.

Even more effective (but more obvious) than the spitter is cutting the ball. Some pitchers will surreptitiously make small cuts in the ball with a razor, push pin, or even sandpaper. When the ball is thrown, the air currents hit the uneven surface and it moves left, right, up, or down, depending on where the cut is. It's a lot harder to sneak a sharp object into the game than a wad of hair goo, but people have still tried. Several sportswriters cite stories of Whitey Ford, in search of another edge, using the rim of his wedding ring to cut the ball. Supposedly, catcher Elston Howard scratched the ball by rubbing it across his shin guard buckle.

For Rick Honeycutt, veteran pitcher for several big-league teams, a favorite method was a thumbtack taped to his finger. Unfortunately it made for another legendary story. After opposing Mariner Willie Wilson hit a double, he noticed Honeycutt's tack when he stood on second base. Wilson alerted the umpires, who came to check it out. In the meantime, Honeycutt had inadvertently rubbed his own forehead with the thumbtack and opened a big cut that bled down his face, so the umpire's "investigation" was pretty short. Honeycutt was suspended and fined (and became the butt of a lot of jokes).

Yankee pitcher Tim Leary, facing the Orioles, used a small piece of sandpaper. When the ump came to investigate, he put the sandpaper in his mouth, leading to a league review of the game broadcast tapes—and endless jokes about smooth tongues and sore throats. Leary was warned but got away with it, at least that time.

You have to wonder, if people put as much effort into trying to win fair as they do into cheating, wouldn't they be more successful at baseball?

Legal versus Illegal and
Fair versus Unfair

Legal and fair are not the same. Legal is supposed to be pretty clear. There's a rule that says you can or can't do something. You are *forbidden* to drive the wrong way down a one-way street or drink if you're underage.

I'm a big fan of sports, not just baseball, so I tend to apply my outlook—fair versus legal—to every game I follow. You *can't* throw a pitch at a batter. You *can't* trip an opponent on the basketball court or hold one on the football field. So you don't. Or do you?

Like a lot of people, I watched the 2017 College Football National Championship game. With two minutes left, Clemson was down by three points to Alabama. Clemson quarterback Deshaun Watson led the team down the field to the Alabama 26-yard line, first down with twenty seconds on the clock. He completed a pass to Jordan Leggett to the 9-yard line for another first down, with fourteen seconds left. The next pass was incomplete; it was now down to nine seconds. On second down, the pass was also incomplete but an interference call put the ball at the 2-yard line and gave Clemson another first down. With six seconds left, Watson rolled out and found

Hunter Renfrow in the end zone for a touchdown, and that plus the extra point put Clemson up 35–31, one of the great upsets of college football. Alabama did everything they could to stop Clemson. Or did they?

The next day, Mike Golic and Mike Greenberg, the ESPN commentators of the *Mike & Mike* show, dissected the game and came up with an alternate strategy. Why didn't Alabama intentionally hold as many Clemson players as they could, drawing a penalty but running the clock down to one second? Because the game can't end on a defensive penalty, their worst-case scenario would have been a tie and overtime. Alabama could have purposely taken the penalty and still have had a chance to win, because the game allows a team to break the rules and accept the consequences. They didn't. Alabama didn't break the rules or incur a penalty, and they lost. Did Alabama do the right thing by not committing a penalty? Fairness is sometimes not so clear-cut.

Head games

What's fair or unfair about getting into another person's head or under his skin? Is psyching somebody out OK?

You're not holding or tripping or throwing spitballs, after all. You're just talking or teasing or giving a funny
look. You're planting seeds of doubt or playing on a fear
or weakness. There are no *rules* against it. When I retired,
I found myself a guest at a dinner at Mar-a-Lago, Donald
Trump's golf resort in Florida. Trump was there, too. We
had met before. I didn't know him well, but eventually
we got to chatting. We talked a little about my career in
baseball, life after baseball, and how I was enjoying my
stay at the resort, and then he asked if I was a golfer. I
told him that now that I was retired from baseball, I was
getting out on the golf course more often. He asked me if
I was any good. I said, "I'm getting better."

Then he said, "I'd like to take your money on the golf
course."

I was a little surprised by this and said, "Well, you
must be pretty good."

"There are golfers that are better," he said, "but I have
it right here," pointing to his head. To him, psyching out
an opponent on the golf course was part of the game.

I didn't want to be a contrarian, but I did find myself
saying, "I like to think, if I win, it's because I'm the better player." I don't want to win just because I'm better at

psyching out my opponent. Donald Trump and I agreed to disagree.

In baseball, I could have tried to mess with every player who got to second base, but I didn't do it. Trash talking in sports in general is common, and in the NBA, it's practically an art form. Michael Jordan is famous for using it off the court, too. When he plays golf, the story goes, when an opponent asks him, "What are we betting?" Jordan answers, "Anything that will make you nervous." This is not a criticism of Donald Trump or the great Michael Jordan. Clearly both have been successful with this approach. It is simply not mine.

The Donald Trump encounter reminded me of a time when I was on the other side of getting psyched out, though I'm not sure it was intentional.

In 1984, I was on a hitting streak. One day we were playing the Angels, and Ruppert Jones hit a double. When he was on second base, Ruppert said, "Cal, you look good with your hands away from your body. You're red-hot at the plate these days. Keep swinging it." That stuck in my head. I started thinking, that must be it—I'm holding the bat a little farther away from my body, and it's working, so I should make sure I do it all the time.

I hardly need to tell you what happened. My next at bat, I didn't get on base, and I immediately went into a slump. Did Ruppert Jones say it on purpose to get in my head? Or was he just giving me a compliment that I overanalyzed? I'll probably never know, but something changed, for sure.

Playing head games is not the way I want to win. I prefer to earn the W by how I play.

Sometimes head games can get personal, as when they're directed at someone else's head, someone you care about.

When my son Ryan was about eleven, he played on a travel baseball team, the Baltimore Buzz. It was tough for him in some ways, having the Ripken name. He struggled at first, and always had other players and parents watching him and expecting him to be a certain kind of player because of his name. At that age, he was smaller than a lot of the other players, so he sometimes struggled just to get in the game. Sometimes he'd trudge back to the bench crying or come home upset, but he hung in, didn't quit, and eventually became a pretty decent pitcher—not fast, but with good control. His travel team had made it to the finals of a tournament in Minnesota, playing a tough team from Florida, and I went out for the game. Ryan was pitching, and he was holding his own, pitching against another kid who was bigger and had a real fastball, especially for his age. In the stands, I could pick up on some chatter, "Is that him? Let's see if he's any good." I felt bad for Ryan but tried to tune it out. If he could, I could.

Midway through the game, the opposing coach stopped the game and went to the umpire, who then called Ryan's coach over. They were huddling about something, so I went over and stood on the other side of the fence, listening. The other coach was complaining that Ryan's motion of raising his front foot up in his windup, then replanting it as he threw, was a balk. Ryan's coach said it wasn't a balk, but the ump wasn't sure. I couldn't help myself and said, "You're nitpicking the rules. That's just his motion. It makes no difference in the game. Let the kids play baseball." The other team's coach looked at me and asked, "Hey, are you a coach?" I replied sarcastically, "No, are *you* a coach?"—my meaning pretty clearly being that he wasn't setting much of an example for kids. Why should a grown man try to get in the head of an eleven-year-old? Is that the way to teach kids to play? Ryan's coach spoke to him, explained it very carefully, and to Ryan's credit, he adjusted his motion and finished the game. My sense of fairness was simple: Let the kids' play determine the outcome; don't let a technicality affect the game.

By the way, Ryan's team won.

Just Show Up

The art of intimidation

There are lots of ways of intimidating the other team—planting stories in the media, on- and off-the-field taunts, illegal hits during and after plays. In baseball, one of the most common ways to get in the heads of the other side is literally by way of the head: the pitcher intentionally throwing at the batter. Just the idea that it might happen can create tension, for the batter and for the whole team. It's human nature to do something—defensive or aggressive—when you sense you're facing a "headhunter." You might back off the plate, anticipating the brushback, and be vulnerable to an outside strike. You might think, *Hey, I'm not gonna let this guy get to me*, crowd the plate, daring the pitcher to throw inside, and then get drilled by a high, tight pitch.

The dustoff, brushback, knockdown, plunker, clunker, headhunter, beanball, and "wild pitch" have been used since the beginning of the game. It's a tactic that is the opposite of fair and one I personally hate, but it's a reality in the game and has been for a long time: Walter Johnson, the all-time leader in the modern era in hitting batters at 205; Sal Maglie, known as "the Barber" for the close shaves he gave hitters; Pedro Martinez, known as Plunk, who was thrown out of twelve games in one year for headhunting; Juan Marichal, whose behavior started more than one brawl; Roger Clemens, who threw a brushback pitch *at his own son* in spring training; Don Drysdale, who was infamous for throwing not one but two knockdown pitches so the batter would know the first wasn't a mistake; and Bob Gibson, who wrote in his autobiography that he threw the nine pitches: "two different fastballs, two sliders, a curve, changeup, knockdown, brushback," and one he actually called "a hit batsman." Then there was Early Wynn, who pitched in the 1950s, and who supposedly said he'd throw at his own grandmother because, he said, "My grandma could really hit the curveball."

Gray areas

I didn't try to get into anybody's head. I wouldn't use the hidden-ball trick. I wouldn't steal the catcher's signs and relay them to batters.

Looking back, though, I realize I did something else that's in the gray area.

When you take a full swing and hit down on the ball, it sometimes hits you in the foot. That's a foul ball.

But if you hit down and it doesn't hit your foot, it's a ground ball, which most likely turns into a dribbler, and you're probably going to get thrown out. There were times when the ball hit my foot and the umpire didn't call it, and there were also times when the ball *didn't* hit my foot, but I acted as if it had, wincing and shouting, "Ow!" I guess I rationalized that the umps had missed a few of those calls so I'd get a few in return. Was it wrong or was it gray?

Back then, they didn't have the technology of instant replay to show what really happened. Speaking of technology, there's a flip side to what it can do to monitor what's fair. It can also be used to play unfairly. Late in the 2017 season, the Boston Red Sox were found to be using an Apple Watch to relay the Yankee catcher's signs from a video booth to the dugout and from the dugout to the Red Sox batters. Stealing signs isn't against the MLB rules, but the use of electronic communication during the game is.

For me, playing fair isn't just what you can get away with; it's what your own standard of fair is. No matter how much you think you've got "fair" figured out, you have to keep reevaluating for new situations, new technology, and new challenges—forever.

Doing the right thing even when no one is watching

In the end, we each have to find our own values, backed by our own reasons, to arrive at what's fair. Going back to my roots—what was ingrained in me as a kid—is the way I judge fair versus unfair. I remember the lessons my dad and mom taught us. Fairness was practically in the very air we breathed.

Every spring my dad, as an Orioles coach, had the job of driving the Orioles station wagon, with a trailer hitched to the back, loaded with all the baseball gear, from Maryland to Florida for spring training. We had a ritual the day before he left: my brothers, my dad, and I would clean the car. Dad was proud of his job and took pride in the fact that his official team car would be in good shape for the annual trip.

However, one particular year, the day before the trip, Dad came home from the Orioles' offices and was beat. He fell into a chair in the den, practically dead to the world. I asked him if we were going to clean the station wagon, and he said that it was probably clean enough.

Leaving him to rest, I went down to the garage and just started wiping down the seats, vacuuming the carpeting, and cleaning the windshield. At my size, it was all I could do to reach the top of the windshield. I heard the door to the garage open and there was my dad, not saying a word, but smiling.

I did it when no one was watching. I was only eight, but the sense of responsibility that he taught me has stayed with me to this day.

It's OK to Be Stubborn

Stubbornness was seen as a positive trait in my little baseball family. When my dad was called stubborn, he stuck his chest out a little farther with pride, and the rest of us—my mom, my sister, Elly, me, and my brothers, Fred and Billy—all had a bit of that, too. I can say unequivocally that I would *not* have had the kind of success I had, or played in all those games in a row, without it.

Cal Sr. said, "Make sure you're good stubborn, not

bad stubborn." In our house, there were two types of stubborn: one meant you had conviction, and the other meant you were being uncooperative. My dad believed in conviction, but only *if* you were sure you were right or believed you had a better way to do things. It's OK to be determined, but it's not OK to be closed-minded. That's the difference between good stubborn and bad stubborn.

My dad was very analytical. It was important to him to know how things worked, even little things, and sometimes he went to great lengths to find out. I was once sitting in a parking lot with him in the middle of winter. I was probably five or six years old. The lot was empty, and my dad noticed that the light poles in the middle of the lot were all a little bent in a similar way. The poles near the outside of the lot were all upright. My dad turned to me in the back seat and asked me if I knew how they got that way. I said, "Maybe they were struck by lightning?"

"All in the same way?" he said, and we kept on thinking of how it could have happened. Eventually he saw a snowplow parked in the far corner of the lot and said, "Aha! I'll bet that's the culprit." There was a maintenance guy painting a curb, and my dad went over to him and asked if he was also the one who plowed the lot when it snows. When he said he was, Dad asked him some questions about how he pushed the snow. Turns out that during the most recent big storm, there was so much snow that the maintenance guy ran out of space so he started making piles around the middle poles. Eureka! The pressure of the snow pushing against the poles had bent them.

The takeaway for me that day, and from lots of encounters like that with my dad, was that I loved his stubborn determination. He just had to figure things out. He always made it clear that you shouldn't make up your mind too fast about what a particular answer is to a problem or puzzle. Instead, you should always get more information, analyze it, reassess, and, above all, be determined to find an explanation. That's how you solve a problem: investigate and ask, and always stubbornly.

My dad carried his stubborn outlook into his job as a baseball coach, too. When his young ballplayers would ask if they had to take infield practice every day, instead of just a few days a week, his answer was always yes. It was clear to him, and he wanted it to be clear to them, that you get good at playing baseball by practice, over and over, not by taking a day off. Daily infield practice meant you'd learn how to anticipate and handle every kind of hit, over and over. Eventually you'd instinctively know when to backpedal for a pop fly, and you'd know when it was hit deeper, between you and the outfielder, and you'd have to turn around and run after it while at the same time being aware of the outfielder's position so as to avoid a collision and yield if he had the better chance. Players said he was stubborn. To this day, I can picture him saying, "Yeah—good stubborn."

I've assumed a lot of my dad's stubbornness; my kids certainly think so. When I decided to help teach my daughter, Rachel, to drive, I definitely used *good* stubborn. My plan was to drive with her as much as I could during the time she had her learner's permit, on highways, country roads, over bridges, through tunnels, in all kinds of conditions—rain, snow, night, day, bright, cloudy, dawn, dusk. That way, I could try to convey my thoughts, my way of dealing with situations, *while driving*, so she could develop better anticipation of whatever might happen.

I soon noticed that she didn't look far enough ahead before we reached traffic lights. I wanted her to learn to anticipate when they'd go from green to yellow and yellow to red, so she could be ready to brake. Her method was to wait until the light turned yellow or red and then brake. I told her it was safer to know the pattern, be ready, and not be surprised. So I invented a game to see who could say "yellow" first when the light changed. I pointed out some clues to look for, like how many cars were waiting at a red light, activity at the pedestrian signal and timer at the crosswalk, and traffic coming across the intersection. The first one to see the light turn to yellow would say it. It worked. To this day, thirteen years later, Rachel and I will be driving somewhere, and she'll say, "Yellow. I beat you."

You have to be a little stubborn to study parking-lot lampposts or fly balls or traffic lights, and then practice until you know just what to do about them—good stubborn. Letting the fly or the light surprise you is being stubborn, too—in a bad way.

I hope I inherited my dad's belief in stubbornness. I hope I've passed it on. Maybe *stubborn* isn't the perfect word to describe this kind of mind-set. *Persistent, detail-oriented,* or *thorough* will do, too. (Trying to find the right word is also a form of stubbornness.) If you have doubts or questions, you need to rethink, recalibrate, and come up with a better way to solve a problem.

Some people might have considered my dad to be closed-minded. To me, he was the most open-minded person I knew. He gathered all the data before he set a course. Then, once he did decide, you couldn't convince him he was wrong . . . because he'd already been open-minded and gathered the information he felt he needed to make his decision.

Good stubborn? I think so.

The streak: good stubborn

I saw a ballplayer's job as an everyday job, not a part-time or now-and-then job. I had a boss, my manager, and I had a defined task—to show up every day, ready to meet the challenges of that day. The boss's job was to decide where and how to put me to work. As a ballplayer, showing up means you're paid to be in the lineup, to be part of the team, day after day. If you can play and you can help the team, then you should play, even if you're banged up.

Of course, there were players who didn't subscribe to that view of the job. They'd find reasons to take a day off—a slump, a groin pull, a sore back, all sorts of non-specific, hard-to-diagnose things. I still laugh when I remember the day one of my old teammates went to great lengths to get out of the lineup. I watched the whole story unfold, from the time he walked into the clubhouse. His name was on the lineup card, and when he saw that, he shook his head, disappointed that he was playing that day. That's when the performance began. He went to the training room and loaded up with ice bags on every part of his body—quads, hamstrings, back, shoulder, you name it—six ice bags in all, probably an ice-bag record. But to take no chances, he paraded, loaded with ice bags, back and forth in front of the manager's office until the manager finally looked up and asked if he was OK. The guy answered bravely, "Yeah, just a little banged up." The manager, who obviously couldn't miss the ice bags, said, "Maybe it's better if we get you a day or two off so this doesn't turn into something bigger." The player shrugged. "OK, skipper, if you say so."

Once out of the lineup, he tossed the ice bags. I always wondered why it wasn't easier to simply walk into the manager's office and say that he was a little banged up and could use a day off. The result would have been the same, but without the charade. I know that an off-day or two can have real value; sometimes, it helps the mental side and gives a player a fresh perspective on the game and on his performance, and sometimes it just reduces muscle soreness and fatigue.

However, I thought the way to be able to keep playing was to play hard and never let up. My plan was always to play through a slump or a tweaked muscle if at all possible. I told a reporter one day, "The time when you have the greatest chance to be injured is the time you let your guard down for a minute, or you don't run out a hit hard, or you try to avoid a collision. It's better to go out and do what you've been trained to do all these years than to try and do something different."

The fact is that, even if I wasn't a hundred percent physically, I could still compete, and I knew there were intangible values I brought to the team by being there every day. Of course, it mattered what the manager wanted to do, too; it had to be right for the team as much as it was right for me. It wasn't just me. Other players, just by showing up, were important to the whole team, too.

Take Eddie Murray. When he was fourth in our lineup, we all felt stable and balanced. All was right with the world with Eddie in the cleanup slot. He could be in an 0 for 50 slump (OK, maybe not quite that bad) and still have an impact on the game just by his presence. When it was time for the opposing manager to make a key decision in a game, he always had to consider Eddie's ability to come through in the clutch. After all, there was a reason he was batting fourth. That opposing manager had to decide whether to pitch to Eddie or pitch around him. If he decided to pitch to him, would he want Eddie hitting from the right side or the left? Eddie was a switch-hitter, and that meant a different pitcher might be needed to try to get him out. I know for sure that I benefited lots of times from Eddie hitting behind me. It could mean I was on the receiving end of a favorable pitcher matchup, and I felt less pressure because all I had to do was get on base and put the game in Eddie's hands. I didn't have to win the ballgame by myself. The whole lineup benefited, because we could all stay in our roles, knowing Eddie was there, hitting number four, as he should be.

My streak wasn't about a record, and it wasn't about boosting Orioles attendance. No—the streak was about a principle; some might call it a work ethic. I was an every-day player; that's what I was hired and paid to do. (Of course, there are players who aren't expected to play all the time, like starting pitchers, relief pitchers, or desig-nated hitters, but those are different jobs. They're doing what they're hired to do, too.) If you're an everyday player, you play every day that you can help the team . . . whether you play baseball or football, teach, or drive a truck. In business, I really value the people who show up every day to meet that day's challenge. It may sound a little old-school, but old-school is OK. You may get nicked, spiked, bruised, banged up, or worn out, but if you're willing and able, you go in to work until your boss takes you out. You play today's game, not tomorrow's. Tomorrow's game will depend on whether you're able to play and whether the boss puts you in. Give your manager or your boss a reason to put you in the lineup by being there ready to play.

That outlook goes all the way back to 1982, my first full season in the major leagues. In '82, I missed a game in Chicago with a fever, and I had also missed one from getting hit in the head by a pitch. The decisions to not play weren't mine; they were the manager's. From then on, I just played every day, as I thought you were supposed to.

Let me be clear. I didn't tell Earl Weaver I was going to play or not; Earl told me. When he put me in the lineup on May 30, 1982, after getting my bell rung, of course he didn't think it was the beginning of a streak, and neither did I. I was just going to work. In fact, the streak wasn't a thing that anyone paid attention to until it hit 1,000 games. As it turned out, starting May 30, 1982, I went to work for the next 2,131 games, which passed Lou Gehrig's record, and I finally sat down after 2,632 games. My managers knew it was a potential record, but they didn't "manage" my streak, because what they all had in common—Weaver, Altobelli, Cal Sr., Robinson,

Oates, Regan, Johnson, Miller—was that their job was to win ball games with the best players they had. Period.

I had nine managers during my Oriole career, and one of them, Frank Robinson, told me, after it was all over, that he had contemplated ending the streak a few times while he was the O's skipper. I was struggling at the plate and he thought maybe he could replace my bat with a better option. At the moment of truth, though, when he sat down to write out the lineup, he thought about all the other things besides my bat that I brought to the team, and he felt he couldn't replace those things. He also said that writing my name into the lineup was the easiest part of his job. It was humbling to hear that, and it stuck with me. I don't think I've ever gotten a higher compliment.

Looking back, I think every manager I played for had his own moment of truth about the streak. The job boils down to putting the team that gives them the best chance to win on the field, and that means figuring out exactly what each player brings to the game in question. My streak was a collection of my managers' decisions, not mine alone. Yes, it was also my stubborn attitude and belief that I could give them what they wanted every game. It's a big commitment, like "for richer or poorer, in sickness and in health, in good times and bad, till death do us part." Well, maybe not death, but I always felt that you had to be hurt pretty bad to not show up for work.

I had an ankle injury in 1985 that nearly kept me out, but not quite, and I had another ankle problem in 1992 that I also played through. The whole team got into a brawl with the Mariners in June 1993; I was right in the middle of it and was pretty sore the next day, but I played. Did I play hurt? Sure, plenty: I had a herniated disk; a hyperextended elbow; ankle, hand, and wrist sprains; bruises from foul balls off the foot, from being hit by a pitch, and from falling into the stands to make a catch; stitches in wounds from metal spikes; oh, and a broken nose at the All-Star Game. That was the strangest injury of all.

It happened in Philadelphia, during the team photo for the 1996 All-Star Game. Chicago White Sox pitcher Roberto Hernández broke my nose, but it wasn't even from a fight. The two of us were in the back row on a platform for the photo, and coming down the steps after the shoot, one of the platforms teetered; Hernández lost his balance, threw his hand back to get steady, and I got the back of a fist across the nose. The trainer kind of manipulated my nose back into place, but it felt like my skin was stretched a little across my face. No matter—I played in the game. It was just my nose, not my arm or leg; I didn't need my nose to play baseball. The next day, I went back to Baltimore to start the second half of the season, played well through the weekend, and then after the Sunday game, I went to Johns Hopkins for a procedure to have my nose put back into place properly.

Maybe it was ridiculous to play with a broken nose; I could have skipped the All-Star Game, gone to the hospital in Philly to get my nose fixed, and focused on being ready for the second half of the season. Instead, I played. It seemed like an easy decision, to be honest. I had a responsibility to the team, to the fans, and to Major League Baseball.

By the way, that was 1996, a year after I broke Lou Gehrig's record. It was just the way I did my job.

During the streak, the Orioles had good years and bad years, and I just kept showing up, ready to play. Some people, even some players, thought the streak sort of took on a life of its own and got more headlines than how we were playing, but to me, the priorities never changed. We had good years, like 1983, when we won the World Series, and not so good years from 1984 to 1988, including our twenty-one-game losing streak in '88. Then we got back to the playoffs in 1996 and 1997. In 1994, when there was a players' strike, people asked me if I'd want to play through it, breaking ranks with the other players to keep my streak going. I said, "No way." My loyalty was with the players and my team. It wasn't about the streak.

I had some good years personally during that time—All-Star Games, Gold Gloves, MVPs, and batting over .300 a few times. I think those were the reasons my managers put me in the lineup, as well as the fact that I never took myself out. My view is, if you have a job, you go to work. If you don't go to work, don't be surprised if you get replaced by somebody who does.

I was an everyday player. I still am.

May the best stubborn win

When I got to spring training in 1995, Phil Regan had just taken over as the Orioles manager. The first two people I saw when I got to the ballpark were Mike Flanagan (my old teammate) and Chuck Cottier, two of the coaches on Phil's staff who had been working with the minor-league players until the lockout was lifted. Once the labor issues were settled, we had exactly three weeks to get ready for the start of the season. Chuck and Mike said, "Boy, Cal, we're glad to see you. Regan's got some different ideas on some fundamental plays." My first thought was, *If you see some problems, why aren't you fixing them? Why are you waiting for me?* After all, they were on Phil's staff.

Sure enough, Phil wanted to put in place a whole new system of defense for bunt plays. I was skeptical, based on Chuck and Mike's warning, but I wanted to first understand what he was trying to accomplish. The first two bunt plays were slight variations on what we already used, but the third play was drastically different. It was an offshoot of something called the wheel play, which the Orioles had discarded a long time ago. (The name comes from sort of moving the infielders around like a wheel to cover the bunt.) The wheel play is risky, and traditionally the Orioles didn't like that kind of risk. The Orioles defense had, up to that point, consisted of an organized effort in which one of the corners (first or third) would charge the bunter, with a simultaneous rotation of players so all the bases would be covered. The three variations we had were the first-base charge play, the third-base charge play, and the pickoff at second. Three plays—and we were always good at both the execution of the three and at disguising them, too.

But Phil liked the idea of a wheel play. In a wheel play, the first baseman, third baseman, and pitcher all charge at the same time. The shortstop covers third, the second baseman covers first, but the middle of the infield is left wide open. The basic idea is to force the out at third, so if it works, you prevent the runner from getting into scoring position. The risk is that if the batter doesn't bunt, or he bunts hard—past the pitcher—a lot can go wrong. The Orioles always wanted to make sure we got an out in this situation, so we'd have the option of walking the next batter and then getting a ground ball and maybe getting out of the inning with a double play.

Phil's version of the wheel play had me as the short-stop starting on third base and the second baseman close to first, which leaves the middle infield open from the start. It also means there's no disguising this play to the offense. As he was introducing his bunt plays, I followed his instructions to a T, but it put all of us out of our usual positions for that kind of play, which meant it was con-fusing and uncomfortable.

After that first practice, I asked Phil if I could discuss the bunt plays with him. We went back out on the field, and I asked him a series of questions about my positioning on his wheel play. I asked very specific things, like, why was it important for me to be on third base at the start of the play? Was he worried that the runner would beat me to third? Was he trying to put pressure on the hitter by telegraphing the play? Phil just kept insisting that the play would work, and he wouldn't really engage my questions. I went at it again, saying that even fast runners like Kenny Lofton or Ricky Henderson had never beat me to third on a bunt play. Again he said, "Cal, I'm telling you, this play is going to work." A manager has every right to put in his plays and carry out his plan, of course, but I left the meeting still concerned. I needed some time to gather my thoughts.

After I worked out and took a shower, I stopped by his office on my way out. I asked if I could make a suggestion. We had only three weeks to get ready for the new season (instead of the usual six weeks, after losing three to the labor problems), so we were going to have to prioritize our efforts. Because we had three of our four infielders returning from last year, and all three knew our bunt plays and cutoffs and relays, and all had executed well last year, wouldn't it make sense to bring the one new guy into our old system instead of all four of us trying to learn a new system, especially in a shortened spring training? I added that if he wasn't satisfied with our execution once we went back north for the regular season, once we'd all worked together, we'd be in a better position to adapt.

First thing the next morning, he called me into his office and told me that what I'd said made sense to him.

He'd keep things the same for now. We went out and executed well and never had to go to a whole new system.

It's OK to be stubborn and even a little argumentative, but you better make sure you have substance in your argument. Sometimes the other person is stubborn, too, and thinks he's right. You can't just hold your ground and wait for the other guy to give in. You have to step back, get objective, and find another approach, one that makes sense to the other person. I was able to win the baseball argument for two reasons: one, because it was from a good, sound baseball perspective; and two, because it was based on common sense applied to the players and a shortened timetable. And the other person, my manager, heard me.

Being right isn't always enough

All-Star Games were great opportunities to share knowledge. Everyone had hitting theories, and I loved hearing them, but I had always thought defense was more straightforward.

For example, I had come to believe I had an advantage when I was deeper in the cutoff position as a third baseman, meaning closer to home plate. Your position is actually dependent on the strength of the outfielders' arms. A stronger arm will throw the ball in on a line; a weaker arm, in an arc. One year, our left fielder didn't have a strong arm, so I'd backed up toward home plate because his one-hop throws would bounce much closer to home. However, I noticed that by backing up to be able to cut off these throws, I could see the runner and third-base coach more clearly. This helped me if the coach signaled the runner to hold or if the runner stumbled rounding third. Then I could make a play on the guy at third or a play on the hitter between first and second, depending on what I managed to see as the throw came in. I could also make a better judgment on the throw to home because I'd be seeing the flight of the ball longer from the outfield and could make sure it was on target, or I could see a race develop between the ball and the runner and could tell if we had a chance at the plate. I could even see the runner who'd hit the ball in my peripheral vision. This real-time data can help you make good decisions.

I was excited to share my discovery with my All-Star teammates that year. I explained the value of being deeper in the cutoff position to my fellow shortstops, Alex Rodriguez and Derek Jeter, and it seemed they understood it perfectly, but when we played, I noticed they didn't use the deeper slot. I asked them about it, and they both said that they were more comfortable doing it their own way. I couldn't really argue with that; they played the game that worked for them, just as I did for me. And of course, both A-Rod and Jeter had great careers. Derek had this great instinct of knowing what was happening behind him, almost as if he had eyes in the back of his head. He would hear the crowd noise change as the play developed and would know something was happening. Over and over, he proved that his instinctual play turned out right. I could hear crowd noise, too, but I wanted to rely on my eyes as much as possible. I liked going out on a ball to the left-center gap with a runner on first. I'd line up for a potential play at home or third. As I was getting into relay position, I'd look over my shoulder to see where the runners were, a good thing to know to help decide where I was going to throw the ball once it came in from the outfield. Then the change in the crowd noise when the runner decided to go for three was music to my ears. I knew the play was at third by using my eyes *and* ears. To this day, I feel I was right about my deeper cutoff positions. The value is obvious, at least to me. But sometimes being right isn't enough. You have to respect the way others get it done. That's not easy for some of us.

It's OK to Be Stubborn

Getting the right players for your team

When we started Ripken Baseball, I had a group of successful businesspeople as advisors. I knew baseball, but I needed to learn about business, too, so we set out to find an experienced executive to run the new company. There were candidates with impressive résumés in business, finance, and entertainment, and they all seemed to want the title of president. After we struck out a couple of times, we took a step back and realized we were looking at candidates with good credentials but not the *right* credentials for our situation (like knowing which pitcher to put in against which kind of hitter.) Just because you've run a large company doesn't mean you know how to talk to kids, or find coaches who understand young athletes, or make parents feel your program is right for their child. We needed someone with business expertise *along with* an understanding of youth sports, someone who "got" youth sports, so his or her priorities were right from the start.

After a lot more searching, we found our guy. His business background was with a major national youth camp and academic baseball showcase, and he had his own consulting business for high-school students in college admissions and recruiting. (And he didn't seem hung up about the title, only the job.) Unfortunately, he was so good, he was later wooed away! But now we have a much better sense of whom we need in our lineup, and we fill positions with that combination of understanding youth sports *and* business always in mind.

In our early days, we outsourced our food and beverage operations, but when we determined that the quality wasn't as good as it should be, we decided to run it ourselves. We needed to choose a leader for the operation, so our folks reviewed more than ninety applicants and narrowed the list down to two finalists for me to meet and make the pick. The problem was, one was clearly the winner, and the other didn't measure up. There weren't really two finalists; the decision was pretty much made, but I wasn't satisfied that we were getting the best we could find. So I asked the team to go back to the applicant pool and come up with a better set of people to choose from, and if they weren't the best candidates after all, I wanted them to reopen the process until we found the right person to lead the team. Finally, after all those interviews, we did find the right person, not the winner from the first round but someone who impressed all of us even more. The important thing was the process. We were thorough, and we took our time. We needed change, and yes, maybe it would be uncomfortable for the people who had been there already to work for the new person, but we were confident we'd gotten the right candidate after taking all that time to comb through all those people.

We learned an important lesson, one that comes right out of baseball: Pick your players and managers carefully, not in a hurry.

When you make a deal, you stick to it . . . even if it's a sticky deal

In the early days, we contracted with Gatorade to supply us with coolers of their sports beverages. Gatorade had become an unofficial symbol of sports, as an energy drink but also with the ritual of pouring it on the winning coaches. The kids loved it, and I loved the authenticity it brings to our experience. A couple of times, though, I went to the coolers and saw there was no Gatorade. Our staff said they'd had complaints from parents that their kids were drinking too much of it, that it was sticky, attracted bees, and was hard to clean up. I had a feeling their problem was mostly the cleanup. I said we had a deal with Gatorade and we were going to live up to it, but to allay the parents' concerns, I told the staff to make sure we had plenty of water for the kids, too. I took a look a couple weeks later and saw that on some fields we just put out water, no Gatorade. I found the guy in charge and told him that when we make a deal, we honor it. I told the coaches that it's part of their job to help educate the kids and monitor their hydration. I said the cleanup was just part of the job. We made a deal. We stick to it.

Don't let stubborn get the best of you

I got thrown out of only three games in the twenty-one years of my career, but I almost got thrown out of more.

Once, because of a rainout early in the season, we ended up with a doubleheader late in the year. The first game lasted fifteen innings, and by the time the second game started, it was pretty late. It seemed obvious, at least to me, that the home-plate umpire, Joe Brinkman, was calling almost everything a strike to hurry the game along and get everybody home. My first time up, I knew I'd have to be aggressive, so I swung at anything close to the strike zone. But when a two-strike pitch was easily a foot outside, I held back—and it was called third strike. I said, "Joe, we all have to be out here. Let's not make it ridiculous." Joe just gave me a hard stare, so I yelled, "What are you staring at?" and he came back with a crude answer. I got a little cruder, and we went back and forth each time we crossed paths, until finally the game ended. Why didn't Joe throw me out? I guess he figured if he had to stay to the bitter end, so did I. He could be stubborn, too.

In another game, Oakland A's pitcher Bob Welch threw a fastball right at me and hit me hard in the wrist. I believed he meant to throw at me as retaliation for a brushback fastball our pitcher had thrown to A's catcher Terry Steinbach.

My wrist stinging, I was on first now, plotting a way to get even. When I got to second base, I thought, since the catcher called the pitches for his pitcher, Steinbach was to blame for my getting hit, so what better chance for payback than a play at home plate. On a base hit to right, I got my wish, hurtling around third base and into a violent collision at home plate. I knocked Terry out of the game. I had gotten tagged out, but not before I had given him a shoulder to the mask. I felt good at the moment, but two weeks later, when I saw him at the All-Star Game, I went over to apologize. Before I could say anything, he put his hands up and said, "There's no need to apologize. I deserved it." That was a classy thing to do, and I still look back and ask myself if I took it too far. Maybe I shouldn't have done it, but . . . I'm stubborn.

Sometimes all it takes is to slow down and take a breath to turn a potentially bad stubborn moment into something better.

One day I was out biking not far from my home, near the Chesapeake Bay Bridge, which goes across to Maryland's Eastern Shore, and I came to a three-way stop. There was a car coming toward the intersection, but it was a way off and heading for one of the stop signs, so I figured it was safe to go. The car didn't stop at all, sailing right through the intersection and almost wiping me out. I hit the brakes and flew off the bike, unhurt but plenty mad. I yelled a string of creative obscenities at the driver, then realized he had gone down a no-outlet road. I could easily catch him. Just as I was getting back on my bike, a woman walking her dog, who'd seen the whole thing, asked, "Are you OK?" Just her stopping to ask how I was and my stopping to think were enough to defuse my anger. Why chase this bad driver? Did I really want to pick a fight with this guy? What's the upside? Instead, I apologized to the lady for my foul language, thanked her for her concern, and rode away.

The lesson is to be stubborn and be right, but also to be smart. Bad stubborn can become dumb stubborn and will get you nowhere, like driving down a dead-end road.

Chapter 5

Baseball Is a Game of Averages . . . like Life

If I've learned one thing—whether it's about batting, fielding, ERAs, net sales, profit margins, ROIs, or happy families—it's this: Consistency wins.

There's no such thing as perfect, but you can aim for a high percentage of success over time. I had five seasons batting over .300. Good NBA three-point shooters hit a little over 40 percent. Pro golfers sink 31 percent of their ten-to-fifteen-foot putts. Today I tally "box scores" in other parts of life to raise my "batting average" of consistency.

Sabermetrics

In the old days of baseball, minor-league scouts used a lot of gut instinct backed by baseball lingo. "That guy is built like a fastball pitcher," they'd say, or "That kid has a hungry look at the plate," or "He's a five-tool player" (hitting for average, hitting for power, running, fielding, throwing), all based on watching a kid in several games but not necessarily enough to see a real pattern. Even though they'd often arrive at the right conclusion, the process was pretty subjective.

Today, due to the spread of the sophisticated math of "sabermetrics," pioneered by baseball geeks Bill James and later Nate Silver, and initially and most notably practiced by Oakland Athletics executive Billy Beane (made famous in the book and movie *Moneyball*), scouting has gotten much more analytical. Scouts now combine their experience with the most relevant statistics. They tend to favor on-base percentage (how often a player gets on base, no matter how he gets there—singles, doubles, triples, line drives, bloopers, hit-by-pitches, or any kind of walk) over pure batting average. To estimate a batter's power, they use slugging percentage (which is calculated by dividing the total number of bases a hitter reaches by how many at bats he has). They factor in a host of other often arcane details. They're using calculus and spreadsheets instead of just their tobacco-chewing gut feel, and thus they've fundamentally changed the way players and their performances are assessed.

Ripken-metrics

When I first made the move from baseball to business, I wasn't relying only on gut feel, but sometimes I may have been guilty of waiting too long, being too understanding of "slumps," before dealing with staff shortcomings. Was that sales guy hitting a patch of bad luck in making partnership deals, or was he going about it wrong? Were our facilities crews keeping the fields in top shape, or were they actually neglecting them? Was that coach teaching the "four pillars" of our organization with passion, or was he kind of sleepwalking through drills with the kids? Were our hospitality people being proactive in making sure families were happy and likely to recommend us, or were they dialing it in?

We changed our tack and established our own box-score metrics. We'd do things like add up the number of initial sales calls made and compare it to the number of follow-up meetings and the number of families who eventually signed up for real, so we could arrive at a true success percentage to measure. We also began spot checks of the fields, stands, scoreboards, dugouts, and equipment to make sure everything was up to our standards every day. We had veteran coaches monitor new coaches, and we did a post-visit survey of every family. Pretty soon it became obvious where our work needed improvement, which personnel still had room to improve, and which ones just needed to be replaced. We didn't act hastily. Instead, we learned to methodically measure outcomes so we knew what to address and how to address it.

Discipline for ballplayers, and for children

From the time I was a little kid of seven or eight, I would go to the ballpark with my father. Back then he was a minor-league manager, but without realizing it at the time, I wasn't just watching him coach, but was also getting parenting lessons.

My dad was a natural parent as a coach. When a young player made a mistake—say, trying to stretch a single into a double and getting tagged out at second—my dad never confronted or criticized the kid at the time. Instead, he kept game charts and put a little red dot next to this kid or that kid's name. After the game, he reviewed his charts, all nine innings—the batting order, hits, strikeouts, fielding stats, runs, errors, pitcher performance—then he made up an index card for each player. The next day, he'd come in and look over his index cards again. Then he'd talk to the player who'd made the mistake privately. He didn't just recite faults. Dad would try to find a positive in the mistake. He might say he appreciated the kid's aggressiveness in going for the extra base and maybe he needed more experience to sense whether or not he could make it. I watched him give these gentle lessons and I internalized them. He was fair and honest, and his teaching style made a big impact on me.

When my son Ryan played high-school baseball, my old Orioles teammate Larry Sheets was a team coach, and I volunteered to help him. During a couple of games, we noticed something negative that some of our other coaches and even a few of the kids on the team were doing, probably with good intentions: they'd get down on their own players when things went badly. For example, if one of our players swung at a bad pitch, it wasn't uncommon to hear a coach yell, "That pitch was over your head!" or "Don't swing at junk!" Sometimes the kids being criticized picked up the negativity and that made their performance next time worse. Sure, the coaches wanted our batters to be better at the plate and not swing at bad pitches, but the way they were handling the correction was all wrong.

The same kind of thing happened when one of our pitchers was having an off day. First the coaches, then the kids on our team, would scowl or shake their heads, or even mutter and groan out loud. All that does is rattle the pitcher more. It can rattle the whole team's confidence, and ultimately it affects how everybody plays. It's infectious. Bad pitches lead to bad fielding, errors lead to more errors, strikeouts lead to more strikeouts, and so on. Losing leads to losing, and we were losing. This wasn't the way to turn it around.

So we changed the way we coached.

Our method was a version of what I'd seen my dad do in the minor leagues. We gave each of the coaches a little book and told them all that whenever they saw a player doing something that needed to be addressed or changed, they should write it down and share it with us later. Larry could then decide how and when to deal with it.

The point was to not bad-mouth the players and not let them absorb negativity. The other team wanted to beat us bad enough; we didn't need to help them. Instead, we needed to not overreact—to calm down and play smart.

The positivity and the dialing down of the temperature worked so well that we turned the season around. In fact, the team won the championship.

I wish I could say it lasted. Players graduate; coaches move on. Two years later, I came back to watch some games, and sure enough, some of that bad behavior was creeping back in.

Bad behavior backfires. Good behavior needs to be reinforced. Whichever one gets more attention is the one that sticks.

When in doubt, underreact

My mom was a master of underreacting. She never disciplined us kids at the time we did something wrong, even though so she had lots of chances. Instead, she waited until things settled down—often quite a while—but the waiting was worth it for her, and for us. The wait times varied depending on the emotions, but when she deemed it was safe to address the problem, she would calmly ask, "Cal, why did you lose your temper and take it out on your brother?" When I was playing in a game and was acting out, later on she'd ask, "Why'd you throw your bat and holler at the umpire?" She'd ask me to think about why I'd done what I'd done.

It is always hard to find a good reason for doing something bad. My mom knew that already but wanted me to realize it, too. Then she'd suggest I find a way for me to tap into the energy source that might have been causing the bad behavior and channel the strong emotions into something positive, like pushups, running around the block, shooting a hundred baskets, or fielding a hundred ground balls. It's amazing how getting busy doing something good can make you too tired to cause any more trouble.

My mom saved her heat for the times we were disrespectful. She was logical and cool unless we failed to respect her; then she was tough. She may have been calm, but she wasn't a pushover.

My mom would have been a good coach.

My dad and mom both had a good way with kids—their own kids, young players, any kids. I'm not saying they were perfect; nobody is, but they were naturals at being parents.

I've tried to be a good parent, but there are still those moments when a misstep can potentially erase the good. In fact, it's like that in all areas of life. You can discourage a player, a child, or an employee with one negative reinforcement.

There was one day in particular that I'll never forget. My son Ryan was young, and that morning he wouldn't get out of bed for school. I first tried to prod him gently, but he kind of kicked back at me, and frankly, I lost it. I grabbed his leg and held it for a second. No big deal—I don't even know if he remembers it—but it bothered me all day. When my dad was a kid, he was punished in the woodshed school of discipline, but he and my mom didn't raise us that way. They were firm but fair, and that's how we tried to raise our kids. When Ryan and I both got home—I from the ballpark and he from school—I sat him down and apologized, promising him I'd never do it again.

And I didn't.

I know a lot of parents say they'd never apologize to their children, because *they* should be in charge, not the kids. I think the people who have real power are those who know they've done something wrong and try to correct it. Kids learn that lesson over time, and it's more important than who's the parent or who's in charge. Mistakes don't get better or go away by denying them or pretending they didn't happen. Facing up to an error quickly and honestly prevents compounding it.

I think I admit when I'm wrong; I certainly try to. (Of course, my kids tease me that when I do apologize, I sometimes make it seem like it's the other person's fault: "Sorry you took what I said that way." Sorry you take it that way, kids!) There's only one thing worse than doing something dumb in your business, on your team, or with your kids, and that's getting in the *habit* of doing it— getting good at being bad. If you yell at your kids and never really listen, you'll be the dad who yells. If you lean on the horn when you're driving, you're the aggressive driver. If you fire people without looking into the reasons why your business is flat or down, then you're the guy who just fires people. It's self-defeating to be the dad who yells, or the aggressive driver, or the terrible boss.

Anger management—a small edge can make a big difference

I didn't lose my temper during games often, at least not by the time I got to the big leagues. In my early days, though, umpires' calls could get me mad, no question.

Umpires are human, and even when they're trying their best, they can make mistakes. But one or two bad calls can make for a bad count that changes the whole complexion of an at bat. Say you have a 1–0 count, one ball and no strikes; the advantage goes to the batter. If the next pitch is another ball and the count is to 2–0, you definitely have the edge on the pitcher. But if the second pitch is a called strike and the count is 1–1, then your edge is gone. The odds that *were* in your favor are now against you just because the umpire made bad calls. That can put you on the defensive at the plate; you could become tentative, overanxious, or hesitant to take a pitch. More times than not, you get *yourself* out that way. So, yeah, from time to time, I let umpires know when I thought their calls were wrong. I let them know loud and clear. Several times I came close to getting thrown out. I took the risk of being thrown out because I was hoping it would make the umps watch more closely, even though it's a basic rule that you can't argue balls and strikes. Their bad calls hurt my chances of getting a hit and hurt my team's chances to score runs and win games. The umps were keeping me from doing my job as well as I could. To me, you just don't take that kind of thing easily, or you shouldn't. Did I handle it perfectly? Probably not. OK, definitely not.

Later, as I matured, I found ways to focus my anger instead of just venting. I was still mad about the bad call, but I learned to settle down, shake it off, block out everything else, and rivet my attention to the pitcher, to his motion and release, and see nothing but the next pitch. I'd still be angry, but I'd try to channel my anger . . . a lesson from mom when she got me to channel my counterproductive energy.

Practicing your profession in public versus private

During one of our long, painful losing streaks, the Orioles' owner came to our locker room and delivered a speech he called "Contest Living." During the speech, he paced around the room dramatically, looking at each of us as if we were members of a jury, as he made his "case." Edward Bennett Williams said certain professionals—trial lawyers like himself, and ballplayers—have to perform their jobs in front of other people, often lots of people, in very public contests. This means the whole world knows when things go badly—in our case, when a team is going through a losing streak. The difference between EBW's world and ours, of course, was that a baseball team can lose sixty times and still win a championship, but for a trial lawyer it's win or lose on each and every case, with no chance to replay it or make up for it the next day or over the course of a season. There's no law season like a baseball season. Eventually, EBW got to his "summation," telling us that what's done is done and we must not dwell on the slump, no matter how many people witness it. He told us to put the losses behind us and move on to the next game and the next, and he charged us up with winning every single game from then on, knowing the whole world was watching. That was just the profession we'd chosen, a very public one. Spectators or not, our job was to win.

That speech on contest living stuck with me over the years. It made me more reluctant to criticize kids, teammates, colleagues, or business partners at the time of a mistake or setback. Even people whose work performance doesn't play out in front of the world—schoolteachers, dentists, waitresses, taxi drivers—know when they're having successes or failures, and it *feels* as if the whole world is watching. Pointing it out, dwelling on it, doesn't make it better. Move past it, tune out the world, focus on your goal.

What wins games—offense or defense?

Besides the streak, most of my baseball stats that people remember are on offense: five seasons batting over .300 and a career total of 431 home runs, 3,184 hits, 1,695 RBIs, and nineteen All-Star Games. Offense is what you *do*. When your team is at bat, you want to get a hit, get on base, advance a runner, get another hit, drive in a run, maybe two, take the lead and build on it. It's true in all sports— run, pass, first down, TD; drive, layup, three-pointer, free throw; ace, slam, lob, game, set, match; drive, putt, par, birdie; pass, slap shot, goal; attack, check, checkmate! Do enough things right and you're in position to win—but only if your defense is good.

My stats in the field, on defense, were as important as the ones at bat, maybe more so: turning 1,565 double plays in my career; fewest errors by a shortstop (three), highest fielding percentage (.996), and 95 games and 431 chances without an error in the 1990 season. Defense is all about being ready, anticipating the play, and knowing what you'll do if the ball comes your way—where you'll move what you'll do if things go differently from what you expect, and all this on *every* play. If offense is making something good happen, then defense is preventing something bad from happening.

That's called balance, and that's what leads to victory.

Avoid the error error

My dad knew he couldn't teach minor-league ballplayers to *never* make an error, so instead he taught them to mentally slow down after they'd screwed up and to do every step from then on carefully and deliberately, to avoid turning one error into two. Don't compound the first mistake by hurrying to try to make up for it.

In Ripken Baseball programs, my brother Billy teaches kids every step: a double play is a catch, a throw, a catch and a throw, and one more catch. This means there are lots of opportunities to make a mistake, but done right, you can also get two outs with one play.

All this brings to mind a player by the name of Jim Gantner, former second baseman for the Milwaukee Brewers, who used to say there are three rules in playing the infield: one, don't panic; two, don't panic; and three, don't panic. In my head, I can still hear my dad's error mantra: "When you drop the ball, don't panic; pick the ball up the first time; don't try to pick it up too fast to make up for the drop and then boot it; just pick it up carefully and surely and then the mistakes are over."

The error mantra applies just about everywhere. If we're building a new ball field at one of our facilities and it seems the infield is uneven, do we regrade it, or do we just keep going, lay down sod, stake out the basepaths, and turn one error into two or three? If you buy a bad stock, do you double down or sell it, take your loss, and move on? If you're late for a meeting, do you drive dangerously to try to make it or leave earlier next time?

Minimize an inning; minimize the chance of losing

Earl Weaver, the longtime Orioles manager, had a pragmatic and highly effective strategy for winning: don't get too far behind. It sounds obvious, but so often it's ignored. At the time, our team had very strong hitting, so we were able to score runs. Let's say we're up by one or two. The other team is batting. They have a man on second base with one out, and the batter hits the ball to left field. The outfielder wants to throw the runner out at the plate, but the smart play many times is to throw to second to keep the hitter at first. This is how you manage the risk. If the runner on second is fast and your left fielder doesn't have a strong arm, the chances of throwing him out are small. If he throws the ball home and the runner is safe, the hitter advances to second base (scoring position), and suddenly your two-run lead is in jeopardy. Because we had strong bats and often the lead, Earl's plan was to force the other team to have to get multiple hits to score a run. If we kept the hits to singles and stopped the base runners from taking extra bases, it was that much harder for a team to catch us.

We use that theory at Ripken Baseball when we're booking our baseball camp spots. We look at the season, week by week, to see how we're doing. Ideally, we'd like to fill up every session, but sometimes we can see by our signups that short of a late surprise, we're going to have a poor performing week or two. We could hope for the late surprise—the perfect throw to the plate—but we'd run the risk of eating a lot of overhead costs, running sessions with too few players, and providing a less than ideal experience for the kids. Instead we could consolidate one or two of those down weeks with a couple of other medium-performing weeks to come out with good, strong weeks. That way we provide the kids a better experience by being with a full group of players, and we do better on our bottom line for the year. We can minimize the bad inning and win the game. What works on the field works off the field.

Offense versus defense in business

When we started Ripken Baseball, like most people, even veteran business types, I tended to look at our "offense." How many deals did we make with sponsors for soft drinks, pizza, hot dogs, pretzels, beer, apparel? How much did we make over costs on those deals? What was our average fan attendance per game? How many kids or families signed up for our programs? These are all valid metrics.

Later, as we got more sophisticated, we also started to study our "defense." Did we resist the temptation to align with sponsors that didn't fit our brand, just for the short-term financial gain? If not, we changed those deals. Did we deliver a great fan experience for the price of a ticket? If not, we set out to improve the experience. Did we make good on the kids' program promises—teaching skills *and* attitudes? We have to.

We took a hard look at every aspect of our business and made sure we were *defending* our company, our concept, our brand. If we committed an error—lost a prospective family—we set out to find out why and tried not to make those mistakes again. Strong offense, even stronger defense.

Like baseball—and just about everything—our business is a game of averages, and our goal is to keep our average as high as we can. When something isn't right, we try to find out why, and then try to fix it.

Chapter 6

Practice Doesn't Make Perfect— Adjustment Does

People who want to be good at what they do practice and practice until their performance is second nature and as close to flawless as possible. But practice is not just doing the same thing over and over; if you want to be great at what you do, you also have to look closely at how you're doing something and make adjustments. Circumstances change, the opposition changes, the times change. You have to learn to recognize the changes and alter your performance accordingly. Nothing stands still, so you can't either.

It took me a long time, but I eventually realized that when things weren't going right, I had to change the way I did things, even if I'd had success in the past doing them the previous way. Some people keep doing what they're doing, hoping that external circumstances will catch up. That's a recipe for a long wait. It's not easy to be objective and honest with yourself, to step back and make adjustments, but all the great players do it.

For pitchers, it's sometimes a tiny tweak in the pitching motion, the way they hold the ball at release, their position on the mound, or a host of other details. For batters, there's the stance, the swing, or the position of the hands on the bat or of the feet in the batter's box. There are a myriad of options.

Then there are big changes. In my case, later in my career, I moved from shortstop to third. At the time, the Orioles wanted to strengthen the left side of the infield, and because I could play both short and third, moving me was the best way to help the team.

Too big to play shortstop?
Play it differently

I'm not sure how many people realize this, but I was drafted as a pitcher/shortstop. At the time of the draft, I was six feet two inches, 180 pounds. Over the next three years, I grew three inches and put on about ten pounds a year. When I struggled at shortstop early on, there was a general feeling that I was too big to play the position. Shortstops are often, though not always, a bit smaller and nimbler, given their need to have great range left and right and to start double plays. Then our third baseman at the time got hit by a pitch that broke his wrist, so I was moved to third base. I did well at third instantly, which seemed to confirm that my size was better suited for the position. I stayed at third until suddenly, in my rookie year, Earl Weaver moved me to short. He wanted to bolster the defense and he believed I could excel at shortstop. Weaver told a reporter at the time, "You never know, Rip might be a great shortstop," which the reporter later referred to as Earl's all-time understatement. All of a sudden, I had to learn to be a shortstop in the big leagues. I could catch ground balls and throw, but learning the particular demands of the position took a little time. I studied other shortstops—Alan Trammell (six feet, 175), Omar Vizquel (five nine, 175), Ozzie Smith (five ten, 150)—all of them great at playing the position, but I soon realized that because of my size I couldn't make many of the plays in the same way they did. They were smaller and quicker and could make acrobatic plays on the run. They could field the ball and turn on a dime with complete control and balance. They all had quick releases and great accuracy on their throws. I had size and reach, plus a strong arm, so I could play deeper. My size also protected me on contact at second base, which meant I could stay in there longer to turn the double play. I used my backhand more, too, and took sharper angles on balls hit more slowly. I learned to spin around to get my body positioned to make a stronger throw on plays to my left. I worked hard at all of this—practice, practice, observe, adjust, then practice more, adjust more. Eventually, I proved that a big guy can play shortstop.

I'm proud that I might have played a role in changing the old stereotype that a shortstop must be small. Guys like Jeter and A-Rod have said that I paved the way for them to be considered at shortstop. As nice as that sounds, I know it's not true; they would have blazed their own trails, given their talent. But I do love the way the position of shortstop is being celebrated and viewed now, with some of the best players occupying that position.

Cal Sr.'s metrics—observation and adjustment

Not only did my dad like to study things to figure out how they worked, but he also used what he learned to find better ways to do things. Keep your distance from traffic in front of you, not just to be safer, but so you don't hit the brakes so hard and wear out the pads, which costs money. Coast toward a traffic light so you don't waste gas.

They're little things, but so are the details of baseball that he also studied in order to find better solutions. The number of feet a runner leads off? Too big a lead and you're in danger of getting picked off. Not enough and you don't get a jump when the batter hits the ball. Back-pedaling for a fly ball versus turning around? Getting your feet set in the box? Your throwing motion? If you don't use all the information you can, you don't take full advantage of your opportunity. Information and analysis—Cal Sr. had his own metrics, before almost anybody else.

Who knows, if he'd written it up, maybe we'd be calling it Calmetrics.

Laundry lessons

I also like to study how things work, even small things.

As a kid, I worked in the clubhouse with my brother Fred when my dad was managing the Asheville Orioles, a double-A affiliate of the Baltimore Orioles. By the time I became a player in the bigs, I knew how the clubhouse functioned. I'd seen the daily routines over and over. A few years later, when I was in the majors, after a game one night, I watched the clubhouse kids put the laundry back in the players' lockers. They piled all the clean laundry on top of a table in the middle of the locker room and put a bunch of hangers on a table next to the clothes. Then one of them would take a hanger, put a T-shirt on the hanger, read the name on the shirt, then walk across the room to that player's locker and hang it up. Then back to the table to start with the next item. This same process was repeated by each of the three clubhouse kids, one garment at a time, back and forth, over and over. Finally, I couldn't take it anymore. I jumped up and inserted myself in the process. "Do you have any rolling hanging racks?" I asked. We found four of them in the laundry room, and we positioned racks on each side of the table. "OK," I said, "let's hang up all the clothes on the racks first. Then we'll sort the clothes by players' locker locations. All the players on this side of the room get their clothes put on these two racks; the players on that side, on those other two racks." Then all four of us (I had joined the crew of three by this point) each had a rack of clothes, two for each side of the locker room. We wheeled the racks to the lockers and systematically dropped the clothes off at each locker. It was faster and more efficient, and best of all, much less work for the kids.

About two weeks later, I was in the locker room late again, and I saw that the kids had gone back to their old routine of one garment at a time. When I asked them what had happened, they told me that, with the new system we'd devised, they were getting the work done way too fast, so the head clubhouse guy would give them extra things to do. The new system was, in a way, too efficient.

A similar thing happened when our team owner, Eli Jacobs, was trying to save money by using a private charter company with smaller jets instead of chartering jumbo jets through an airline. It seemed like a good idea until they got to the details. Because the planes were smaller, they had to remove the extra fuel tank to make room for all of our equipment. That didn't mean we were in danger of running out of gas, but it did mean we had to get gas more often. We couldn't go coast to coast without refueling, and even with the savings on the cost of the jumbo jets, refueling costs money. And the longer trips cost us all time and meant that we arrived more fatigued.

The answer was to use jumbo jets for long hauls, and use smaller jets only for short trips. We adjusted.

Tape ball, the antislump game

Sometimes the best way out of a slump is to find a way to take your mind off of it and keep you sane while you wait out the bad stretch. When the O's were deep in our 1988 losing streak, I created a game to get our heads out of it, even if only for a few minutes—tape ball.

My version of tape ball was a variation on what we did when we were kids. Back then, we could make almost anything into a baseball—a balled-up paper cup, a napkin, an old newspaper, or best of all, a tennis ball. We'd wrap the ball with tape and then play a version of baseball that was less likely to break windows. In the case of our slump, it was our *spirit* that was breaking. From opening day on, for more than a month, being on the field was no fun. One day in the Metrodome in Minneapolis, after loss number nineteen, I was in the locker room, still in full uniform, and I wandered into the training room, picked up a sanitary sock (the sock that goes inside a baseball stirrup sock) and idly rolled it into a ball. Then I found some adhesive tape, the kind you use to wrap a bandage on your ankle, and wound it around and around the sock, shaping it into a soft, squishy ball. I made a couple more tape balls, grabbed a fungo bat, gathered up some other down-in-the-dumps players—Rene Gonzales, Joe Orsulak, Ben McDonald, my brother Billy, and a couple more guys, plus a bunch of the clubhouse kids—and we went back down onto the field. The place was empty, but the lights were still on.

First, we made a "field." We turned home plate around so it became second base, with the backstop behind us as the outfield fence—kind of a miniature diamond in reverse, so the ball couldn't get far away from us. Then the guys on our team would play against the clubhouse kids, usually four on four. I was pitching, and the more we played, the softer the ball got, so on each pitch I'd squish it flatter and flatter until it was like a pancake. That way I could get it to go up or drop down a lot, almost like a Frisbee. The kids would shout back calling it a saucer ball (like a flying saucer). We'd all be laughing, playing this weird, invented game.

For the professionals, it was a way to reconnect to the innocent fun of the game. It would be a better story to say that the next day we broke the streak because of tape ball. Unfortunately, that wouldn't be true. Nevertheless, I think we all felt more grounded and less stressed. We lost the next two games, but we played well. Then on our first day in Chicago, April 29, we won 9–1, and the streak was over. And that was pretty much the end of tape ball.

Sometimes you need a new perspective on an old habit to break out of boredom, to bring back the joy, or to just win a darn game.

The evolution of Ripken Baseball—from minor-league teams to youth baseball

When we started out, we had a two-part plan: the minor-league/pro-team part and the kid/amateur part. My passion always was and still is the amateur side.

We had early success with our minor-league team, so we set a lofty goal to buy ten teams in ten years. That proved hard to accomplish, but we did buy two more teams fairly quickly. Originally, in Aberdeen, we had a partner who wanted to take an independent baseball–league approach— teams having no affiliations with big-league clubs. But my brother Bill and I, and our careers, were products of the affiliated model—minor-league teams connected to major-league teams—so we thought that would make a better product for fans and a better business. Those minor-league teams would sign the best up-and-coming baseball players— those with the potential to make it to the big leagues—so fans would come out and see them. The major-league teams pay the players' salaries; the minor-league teams sell tickets, sponsorships, food, and merchandise.

We'd never run a baseball team before, but we had grown up in and around minor-league baseball. We made tons of mistakes, but we learned from each one. It's like facing a pitcher for the first time. Maybe he drops a couple of nasty curveballs on you and then finishes you off with a high fastball for a strikeout. The next at bat, you come to the plate smarter, with a better idea of the pitcher's stuff.

Fast-forward to our next step. Even though we had

some success on the pro side, we decided to focus on the kids' side. We feel we have a real advantage in the kids'-baseball space—our baseball credibility. It came initially from our father, who spent a lifetime coaching and teaching baseball, but it also came from our own success in the sport. We have player-experience credibility with parents, coaches, and players. The youth side involves running tournaments, camps, and clinics, teaching the game, and giving kids a big-league experience, with replica fields of big-league parks with major-league amenities.

Now, scaling our business, learning from each experience, and opening kids' complexes throughout the country, we can constantly tap into our three successful existing models. You could say that we've evolved to our strengths—practice, practice, observe, adjust. Most important, the youth side of the business is where our hearts lie.

Don't just hire the right people

In managing and growing Ripken Baseball, I've borrowed heavily from the management philosophies of my friends and business associates—Steve Bisciotti, founder of the personnel company Aerotek (now Allegis) and owner of the Baltimore Ravens football team; Kevin Plank, founder and CEO of Under Armour; Robert Altman, founder and CEO of ZeniMax Media; and others. Conventional wisdom says hire the right people and just let them do their jobs, but my go-to experts have taught me that after you hire the right people, you're only halfway there. The other half is setting goals and making clear to all of them what they're to do—in our case, build the brand, set up sponsorship partners, and work with coaches or parents. If you don't clearly direct the people beneath you, you can't expect them to execute.

We are hands-on managers, and we make no apologies for it. It's how we've grown, and it's how we plan to grow further: get the right people, and give them goals. You'd be amazed what people can do if you give them the respect they need to believe they can succeed.

The changeup—in the pitching rotation or in a business sales pitch

Mike Flanagan was the pitching coach under manager Ray Miller, and Mike and I were pretty good friends. One day I asked him why the starters were getting pulled from games so early and the relievers were getting all the innings—one-third of the innings for starters, two-thirds for relievers, the opposite of what you'd expect. Flanny didn't agree with this strategy, but he thought it would be better if I went to Ray Miller to suggest a different approach.

Late one night after a game, I walked by Ray's office. He was still in his uniform, and he was alone. I went in to chat with him, and the floodgates opened. I let him vent for a while, about starters not giving him innings, about our offense not scoring runs in the clutch, and about not closing out games. Eventually he got it all out, and we sat there in silence for a while.

Then I asked, "Why is Jesse Orosco on our team?"

Ray said, "He's supposed to get the best lefties out."

I said, "Right, so how about using him only against lefties?" Then I asked, "Why is Mike Timlin on the team?"

Miller said, "He's supposed to be our closer, but if the game is tight, I can't wait."

"Then only use him in a situation that calls for a closer. Don't use him in a tie game in the seventh or eighth."

We also talked about Arthur Rhodes, another pitcher I thought we could have used in a better way. He had won ten games out of the bullpen two years in a row. He could fill in for two, three, or even four innings, and he had really good stuff, which could get righties and lefties out equally. If we got a lead with Artie pitching, then we could turn the game over to the rest of the bullpen. Instead, Ray was using Arthur all over the place, in all kinds of situations.

One player at a time, we went through the whole bullpen and talked about using these guys only for their specialty, which naturally would mean leaving the starters in longer and letting the relievers rest up. Sometimes you might have to tell a pitcher that he has to stay in for five or six innings, even if he's gonna get his head beaten in. Sometimes the pitcher will get the game back under control. Plus, no amount of extra bullpen sessions will make up for reducing their innings.

It must have made sense to Ray, because damn it if he didn't do it, and it straightened things out. We started getting more chances to win, and we started winning. Ray had told us back in spring training that the key to our success was to put people in a position to be successful. He just needed a gentle reminder.

The same idea works outside of baseball. Stay with your "starters," your strengths, before going to your "relievers," your fallback plan. Then when and if you do make a change, adjust carefully.

In our baseball business, we've tried to instill the same lesson. When we're making a presentation, sometimes at the first sign of a question or pushback from a prospective vendor or partner over the terms of a deal, we'll be tempted to back off and take less in the deal—that is, go to our relievers. If we throw in the towel too early, we send a message that we aren't confident in our brand or our fan base, or that we feel the vendor can take advantage of us. Instead, we remind ourselves to give our starters a chance to win before we go to our bullpen. If we're getting major pushback on a proposed deal, we might look at other ways to construct the deal. We like our people to listen, observe, and adjust carefully when needed. There are often creative solutions—different terms or prices— that will work better than just sacrificing everything for the immediate deal.

Bud Selig—guiding baseball from its low point to its heights

One of the most successful adjustments I've ever seen came after the baseball strike of 1994. The strike was a near-disaster for the game, with a 232-day work stoppage and the cancellation of the remaining season and the World Series.

Bud Selig was the MLB commissioner at the time, and there were those who said he was presiding over the demise of the game. With so much criticism, the catastrophic strike could have been the end of his career. Instead, Bud looked long and hard at what had occurred and why, and he made significant changes. The introduction of the wild-card playoff game, the official merging of the American and National leagues under the office of the commissioner, along with interleague play and true revenue sharing— all these steps eventually led to record attendances and a 400 percent increase in revenue. Selig also faced up to another reality by commissioning the Mitchell Report on performance-enhancing drugs and drug testing, and by subsequently instituting a treatment program. In 2015, Bud Selig retired with a reputation as one of the best, if not the best commissioner in the history of the game. Some say he saved the game, including some of the same people who had said he was overseeing its downfall.

The key thing was that he looked at what had gone wrong, and he adjusted.

World Series of adjustment—
Francona versus Maddon

When I was on the Orioles, I liked watching and studying and playing against the best players, the best teams, and the best managers. It was always fascinating to me to see how and why they won. The truth is, you can have a team full of expensive superstars and still lose. It happens in all sports. Think of the Brazil team, in a World Cup semifinal, with Neymar da Silva Santos Júnior, Willian Borges da Silva, David Luiz Moreira Marinho, and a host of other great players on their squad, still losing 7–1 to Germany . . . in Brazil.

A big part of the problem in that game was management, as in baseball and all sports and work in general. The Brazilian team wasn't set up to win that game. They didn't focus on defense properly. In my sport, you can go acquire the best players available, but if you don't put them on the field with a strategy, a coherent and well-thought-out game plan—including things like when to bunt, when to hit and run, whom to put in the batting order and where, whom to make the designated hitter, whom to start and whom to have ready as short reliever and closer, what pitch to throw to this or that guy, when to steal and when not to—without all this in place, you can't win. If your initial game plan is working, stick with it. If it isn't working, you need to adjust to a contingency plan and make it work.

If you're looking for proof that superstars don't always win, look at the 2016 major-league results. The two highest-paid teams of superstars were the Dodgers, with a $220 million payroll, winning their division but losing the NL pennant, and the Yankees, at $213 million, finishing fourth in their division. The two teams that did play in the World Series were the Cubs, fourteenth in payroll at $116 million, and the Indians, twenty-fourth in payroll at $86 million. Both the Cubs and the Indians had brilliant game management. The Indians manager was Tito Francona, who, don't forget, had broken the Red Sox' eighty-six-year World Series drought. The Cubs manager was Joe Maddon, the guy who had previously led the Tampa Bay Rays, with the second lowest payroll in baseball, to the 2008 American League pennant. Sure, there were great players on both of those teams, but their biggest assets were great managers who executed brilliant plans.

Both teams in the 2016 series had suffered through championship droughts. The Cubs hadn't won since 1908, and the Indians hadn't won since 1948. The Cubs came into the series as the favorites, with the edge in pitching-rotation depth, defense, bench strength, and power hitting. But Cleveland had some good weapons, too, including excellent relievers—Andrew Miller and Cody Allen—and probably the best starter in baseball, Corey Kluber. Francona knew he had to get his three wins from Kluber and just one from anybody else, but he had to be very careful about using Miller only when he needed him most—not too soon or too often—so he'd still be there to call upon later in the series. That part worked—with Miller in the game, Cleveland won games one, three, and four. But the Indians lost games two, five, and six when Tito didn't have his top relievers available. That meant the series went all the way to game seven. Francona was ready with his three best pitching weapons—Kluber, Miller, and Allen, but Kluber was off this game. What a time to garner no strikeouts, a career first. Miller wasn't much better, giving up four hits, something he hadn't done in five years.

Meanwhile, Maddon had his own plan. Just when it seemed the Cubs were going to keep their curse going, Maddon put in his closer, Aroldis Chapman, for a save in game five. Then he worked his batting order to get the team ahead 7–2 in game six, and brought Chapman in for the seventh, eighth, and part of the ninth, with the Cubs up by seven, thereby bringing the series back to even.

The problem was, Maddon had worn Chapman down heading into the deciding game. In game seven, with a 6–3 lead in the eighth, and the Cubs six outs away from their first World Series win in over a century, Maddon put Chapman in. To Francona's credit, after Brandon Guyer hit an RBI double, he saw Chapman's fatigue and believed his center fielder, Raj Davis, was overdue for a hit, and he was right. Davis hit a two-run homer to tie the game at the end of nine innings. To add to the drama, the game was then delayed by heavy rain. Finally, going into the tenth inning, just about out of pitching miracles, Maddon turned to his batting power. He got the go-ahead double from Ben Zobrist and an RBI single from Miguel Montero. Cleveland got up to bat and wouldn't die, putting the tying run on base. Maddon went to the bullpen for Mike Montgomery, and he got the final out in the tenth inning. The Cubs had finally won the World Series again.

In the end, Maddon's team won, but it was a battle of master strategists and master adjusters, not superstars.

Just Show Up

You can change only what you can see

Sometimes you have to sit in the back of the team bus to see what's going on.

All the practicing and adjusting in the world won't help you unless you have clarity of vision. Everything needs a context, and you need to know how you're doing compared to how you're expected to do.

When you ride back from a game in the bus, you're surrounded by people from all over the world, of different colors, from all different social and economic backgrounds, with different levels of education. You have no privilege or free pass. If you played well, everyone knows it; if not, everyone knows that, too. Did you get a hit? Did you make the right play in the eighth inning? Did you turn the DP? Did you drive in a run? As the late Senator John McCain said, "The facts have a way of being persistent." Taking a real or metaphorical seat at the back of the bus will help you reassess and change if need be. There's no hiding back there.

In sports, there's what's called the sophomore jinx. A lot of players falter after a good rookie year. Your opponents figure you out. Your surprise factor is gone.

I was Rookie of the Year in 1982, hitting 28 home runs. I had heard of this sophomore jinx, and I was determined not to have that happen to me. I knew the league would know me better now and would make adjustments, so I had to be ready to readjust to their adjustments. It was clear to me pretty quickly that pitchers were not going to give in to me, and they went out of their way not to fall into a pattern. Accordingly, I had to prove that I could hit all the pitches in all the counts.

I'm proud to say that in my sophomore season, I kept my fielding percentage almost identical at .970, hit .318 with 27 home runs, and was voted MVP of the league. That's the value of seeing things clearly from the back of the bus and adjusting when necessary. If I'd tried to coast or do only what I did in that first year, I could have slumped, but I reworked my perspective, and it paid off.

When you learn to adjust like that, you gain control over your performance. You have perspective; you have context. You control the game, the other team, the other player, the other company, the other candidate, rather than being controlled. The competitors have to adjust to you, and there's no better feeling than knowing *you've* forced a change in what *they* do.

Perseverance: on the field and online

A few years ago, I was invited to give a talk to the executive team at Cisco, the IT and networking conglomerate. At the time, my go-to speeches focused on teamwork and leadership, but Cisco wanted one on perseverance. After all, I broke the record for most consecutive games played.

I went out to Colorado, the site of the conference, three days early, and locked myself in one of the cabins determined to define *perseverance*. The first day I drew a total blank, but halfway through the second day, a lightbulb went on.

I remembered a conversation I had had with Derek Jeter at an All-Star Game. Derek had asked me if there was a secret to playing all those games in a row, and I'd admitted that in fact there was no secret at all. I genuinely had no words of wisdom for him. He seemed disappointed, and the encounter left me feeling that I needed to come up with a better answer.

A few weeks later, a reporter asked me what qualities a player would need to have to break my record. I did my best to respond to the reporter on the spot, and I remember thinking that what I'd told the reporter could've been the basis for a better answer to Derek. I realized there were six things that came together to define perseverance: patience, discipline, perspective, tenacity, relentlessness, and unwavering pursuit.

I remembered those six factors on that second day in Colorado and based my speech on them. Here's how I see them:

Patience. To understand patience, compare it to impatience. One of the things I love about baseball is that it takes a long season of 162 games to even get to the playoffs. No matter how impatient you might be, baseball isn't. You can't be in a hurry; hurrying won't get you there. You can't rush being a good boss, either. You have to study your team, learn your business, practice good management, and repeat.

Discipline. Discipline is resisting the temptation to take a shortcut, no matter what you do. It's fielding grounders, left, right, up the middle, again and again. It's time in the batting cage, pitch after pitch, swing after swing, sometimes after everybody else has gone home. If you run a business, you have to double-check the numbers even when it's boring. As my dad would insist of us kids, you have to shovel the snow so the whole sidewalk is clear, not just a little path (even when it's going to snow some more.) It's doing what you did the day before to make sure you're doing it just as well today.

Perspective. That back-of-the-bus view—that's where you'll see most clearly. It's hard in the middle of a ballgame to get perspective, but it's crucial. It means seeing where the game is going and seeing who is playing well and who isn't. It's hard in the middle of any workday, but it's important to take a breath and look at what's happening, to focus not just on the job in front of you, but also the one a few days and weeks ahead.

Tenacity. Tenacity means never letting go until you reach your goal. When I was fielding, I often found myself diving for a ball that was probably out of reach because maybe, just maybe, I could stretch and get it. The same goes for business. How do you pitch for a client who seems out of reach? Well, you keep at it, because you never know. You might reach and get it.

Relentlessness. You need to go after what you want with no letup, no interruption. For me, that meant playing inning after inning, game after game, even when my elbow was bruised or my nose was broken—not because I was going after a record but because the real record was being there for my team. You don't want your customers to take a day off from you, so you need to be there for them day in and day out.

Unwavering pursuit. It wasn't just about playing all

those days in a row; it was also about running out an almost sure groundout for that 1-in-10 or 1-in-100 chance that I could beat out the throw. Think about the customer that your competitors are ignoring. Couldn't you give them the service they need? Being persistent—yes, stubborn—and noticing the little stuff every single time, not once or twice, is the essence of unwavering pursuit. My dad took extra time with everyone from the mailroom to the kit room. Pursuit, unwavering pursuit.

That's my definition of perseverance. If you're reading this, Derek Jeter, that's my answer about the streak. It's all about building and repeating good habits until they become automatic. If you hit a wall, find a way around it. Adjust and readjust.

Not that Jeter needed my help.

Chapter 7

Have a Mentor, and Be One, Too

We're all surrounded by people wiser than us—parents, friends, teammates, coaches. The key thing is, we have to pay attention to them. I've had the benefit of great mentors in my life—my father, teammates, good friends— and have tried to be a good mentor myself, to teammates, to my children, to my friends. I've tried to pass on the experience and wisdom I've gained to others. I think that's our responsibility in life, and in sharing what you know, you keep learning.

Father, guru, coach, role model

We came home every day to our mentor, Cal Sr., but he wasn't only mentoring us. During the day every season, we shared him with his teams. During the first fourteen years of my life, he was a "dad" to all the guys on his teams, a father figure to every one of his players. He got calls in the middle of the night about a homesick kid, a skirmish in a bar, or something else. He believed his responsibilities went beyond what happened on the field. He was shaping young men. He was a pitching coach, a hitting coach, a fielding coach, and a life coach.

My dad didn't have high standards only on the baseball field. He had high standards for us at school, when we cut the lawn, or in whatever it was we were tasked with doing. But my father always explained the "why" of doing things right; it wasn't just mindless work to him.

Teach and learn; learn and teach. You learn from teaching as much as from being the student. Having the good intention of completing a task is not nearly as important as actually doing it. Everyone can promise to do a good job; someone has to go do it. Why don't you?

Mom-mentor, the gentle enforcer

My dad knew what he believed in and laid down the law. My mom never contradicted him, but she knew more about emotions, the ups and downs of her kids, when to dive in and when to back off. He stated; she understated. He was passionate; she was compassionate. They believed in the same things, but they instilled them in different ways. The combination made it all work.

Brooks Robinson

As I got older as a player, my popularity with younger fans seemed to grow, and for a long time I couldn't work out why. My stats were declining; I wasn't one of the handsome, whiz-kid players; I didn't appear in commercials staring at the camera like a hot young superstar. Fans didn't necessarily buy sneakers because I wore that brand. Still, each year, I would find that after games there would be a long line of kids wanting autographs; letters and cards kept arriving from young people. What was going on?

When I was young, my dad had always held up Brooks Robinson as a hero in our house. The "Human Vacuum Cleaner," as he was nicknamed, third-baseman Brooks was a brilliant defensive player; he won sixteen consecutive Gold Gloves at his position—and he only ever played for the Orioles. (It didn't hurt that his middle name was Calbert, either.) More than anything, though, my dad held Robinson up as a role model because of how he comported himself off the field, as much as on. There was never a hint of scandal with Brooks; he was a stand-up guy who showed up for work, made the plays he needed to, and then showed up the next day to do it again. Growing up in the Ripken household, Brooks Robinson was someone we looked up to, revered, someone our dad said was a hero. I wonder if that's what was happening in my case. Parents were pointing me out to their kids just as Dad had pointed out Brooks Robinson to us. I was just this guy at third base or shortstop who showed up day in and day out to do his job. I wasn't the flashiest superstar, but for people who themselves had to go to work every day, rain or shine, I was something of a role model, or at least someone the kids heard a lot about, and that's why they'd wait for me after the game.

I guess the point is that it's amazing what children take from their parents. You might think they're not always noticing what you say and do, but kids don't miss much. Picking the right role models matters; pointing out the right way to live matters; living by example matters. We understood that Brooks Robinson was a hero for the way he played and the way he lived. We wanted to be him, to live the right way, to pass on the essential lessons in working hard, doing the right thing, and being someone who lived a good life. Dad didn't have to go on about why Brooks was a hero; he just picked him and pointed him out to us. Think about whom you admire, and why, and what your kids take from it. It matters.

So who is *my* Brooks Robinson?

I've been lucky enough to spend some time in the last few years with Archie Manning. My wife's daughter, Madison, is a senior at Ole Miss, and we often go down to visit. Archie, who went to school there, often travels back to his alma mater for football games, and on off-weeks in the NFL schedule, sometimes Eli, his star quarterback son, joins him, too, so I've gotten to know the family. It's clear to me that Archie is a Brooks Robinson kind of figure: does the right thing, in the right way, quietly and effectively living a life that's a model for his sons and others. It's not just the fact that his sons—Cooper, Peyton, and Eli—have all been successful in their chosen careers and overcome adversity in their own ways. It's that Archie's example continues to shine; you only have to spend a little bit of time with him now, long after the success of his boys—to know that he's a Brooks Robinson kind of guy.

Everything starts with the "foundation"

I don't think my dad ever used the word *mentor*, but even if the word was unspoken, the idea, the belief, living it, shone through in everything he did. What he did say often, was, "What you do today is practice for how you will live tomorrow."

That's what motivated Billy and me to establish the Cal Ripken Sr. Foundation. It's no surprise that my mom made sure our mission statement was true to Cal Sr.: *The Cal Ripken Sr. Foundation helps to build character and teach critical life lessons to at-risk young people living in America's most distressed communities.*

The foundation aims to embody his values as a coach

and mentor: leadership, work ethic, personal responsibility, and healthy living. It funds programs for at-risk young people. One of our programs is called Badges for Baseball, in which we essentially teach police officers to be baseball coaches, and they form bonds with kids in tough communities. Mentorships are formed, and the law enforcement officers are seen in a different and more positive light.

My dad would have said, "Nice start. Now keep it up."

Managers or mentors or both?

Nobody said mentoring is easy. It's an art more than a science. It should flex with the situation and the person.

A lot of managers in the big leagues say something like, "I'm a fair person, and I'm going to treat you all fairly, but that doesn't mean I'm going to treat you all the same."

If you're a player who's playing regularly, you've earned some consideration that maybe somebody else hasn't earned, at least not yet. If a guy is playing in 162 games, maybe you don't ask him to stay on the field as long for practice, or maybe you cut him some slack by letting him come in later the day after a night game. You might not give that same leeway to a younger player who needs to have his habits shaped and his discipline developed. That, too, is a form of fairness.

Eddie Murray, a mentor of few words

When I came to the Orioles, Eddie Murray took me under his wing. I was a kid and he was a veteran, even though he wasn't much older than me. I think Eddie felt something for me because my father had taken a special interest in him in the minors. Dad had been instrumental in encouraging Eddie to switch-hit.

Eddie Murray has had a reputation for being introverted, not a high-fiver or glory seeker, quiet, maybe even a bit shy. The truth was, Eddie was outspoken when he was comfortable. He could be funny, in a dry, low-key way. He taught me how to conduct myself in the big leagues, when to talk to the press—something he didn't do much of—and what to keep to myself. I didn't mind talking to sportswriters as much as he did, but I learned from Eddie to measure every word, so I wouldn't be misinterpreted.

Eddie was not an in-your-face, "I'm telling you what

to do" kind of guy. As a mentor he said his piece, and if you wanted to listen, that was fine. If not, that was OK, too. I used to say he whispered his wisdom, so you had to lean in to learn it. Wisdom can be like that. It's there if you pay attention.

Adversity, the teacher

Ron Darling Jr., former pitcher for the Mets and my broadcast partner on TBS Baseball, has a truly inspirational father. Ron credits a lot of what his dad gave him to what his father never got from his own parents. Ron Sr. was completely abandoned at age four and was then taken in by one farm family after another, until he left and joined the US Air Force. Stationed in Hawaii, he met his wife-to-be, whose own mother had died in childbirth. Ron's father said his parents were a pair of "stray dogs," an ideal match. Both somehow derived positives out of their challenging backgrounds, striving to give their children the love and attention they'd never experienced. They raised their four sons in a disciplined but caring household, with homework and bedtime nonnegotiable. They instilled strong values and set high standards. If

Ron seemed to have nothing to do, his mother didn't send him off to watch TV; she took him to the library. It must've have worked; he went to Yale. To support a family of six his father sometimes held down multiple jobs, and not glamorous ones. Ron remembers going with him to do garbage collection at the crack of dawn. But instead of regretting those early mornings, he valued them as special time with a wise man and father. Ron's father somehow found time to also be his Little League coach, but his mother was the one who practiced with him. She'd played third base on the local softball team and passed her skills on to her sons.

At seventy-two, Ron's mom is still playing catch with him. Apparently, she can still handle his fastball.

Would Ron Jr. be the man he is today without the challenges his parents faced? Would he have learned the same lessons? Would he be passing them on to his kids? Is misfortune a better teacher than good fortune? It's hard to wish for suffering, but it's also hard to argue with lessons born of adversity. When I hear young kids complain about working too hard, getting up too early, having demanding teachers or bosses, not having enough money, or not having time off, I often think of Ron Darling and his parents.

Have a Mentor, and Be One, Too

Sometimes a mentor is just someone who takes your side

Rookie hazing is a tradition in sports, but I don't like it.

I think by the time you get to the big leagues, you've paid enough dues, working your way up through high school, college, AA and AAA minor-league ball—you're not a rookie anymore. For the most part, the pranks are harmless—making newbies carry bags for the veterans, nailing their shower shoes to the floor—silly stuff. Once in a while, though, the pranks go too far.

One day in Milwaukee, pitcher Armando Benítez came in after a tough game and found only a woman's dress in his locker. Other guys who were considered rookies had been given the same dress and had walked out to the bus wearing it, to the razzing of a few straggling fans. Armando sat at his locker just staring at the dress and wouldn't move, but the bus wouldn't leave until all the players were on it. Some of our guys—Davey Johnson, Rafael Palmeiro, Robbie Alomar—tried to convince him to wear the dress and get it over with, but still he wouldn't move. It was humiliating.

I decided to give it a try. I sat with him quietly for a while, and then I said, "I wouldn't do it either." He was surprised to hear that. I said, "Hey, tell you what. We're not playing until tomorrow night. Why don't you and I take a separate flight?" Armando was thinking about it when Davey Johnson, who'd gotten so annoyed, convinced the guys who did it to return Armando's clothes. Armando put them on and walked out to the bus.

I didn't think any more about it, but Armando did. Evidently, the little trust we had created for a few minutes stuck with him and helped build a rapport between us that lasted. Well, that trust, plus one more incident.

A couple years later, in a game against the Yankees, Armando couldn't control his emotions after giving up a grand slam to Bernie Williams and decided to take it out on the next batter, Tino Martinez, drilling Tino in the middle of the back with the next pitch. That started a good old-fashioned baseball brawl. Daryl Strawberry came at Armando, umps tried to break it up—the whole thing. After a lot of punches and curses had been thrown, it settled down.

A lot of people, even guys on our team, were pissed at Armando. After the game, he sat in front of his locker, long after most people had left, silent and staring, just like during the hazing incident. I went over and sat with him, quiet at first. Then I said, "It's just not right to drill someone because you gave up a homer. But you might be the only one with guts enough to do it here in Yankee Stadium."

This got him smiling, and he got dressed. I had backed him when he had done the wrong thing and knew it was wrong. All he needed was somebody to tell him to learn from his mistake and move on.

Two years later, after he was traded to the Mets, he came looking for me at spring training in Port St. Lucie, Florida. He told me he remembered what I'd done for him and handed me a diamond-and-gold ring he had made with my number 8 on it. He said he appreciated my being there when he needed it.

You don't always get noticed for what you do. That's not why you do it. You do it because it's right. And you hope someone will do it for you. But Armando Benítez made me a ring, and I treasure it.

If everybody is a kid, who's the mentor?

I never felt like a rookie. I grew up around the game with my dad being a coach, so it was all familiar territory—up days and down days, riding buses, living on the road, workouts, drills, locker-room life, unglamorous minor leagues, being alone a lot.

But for plenty of guys I came up with, this was their first time away from home, and they got homesick. Some guys got so discouraged, waiting to make the big dance, that they quit, or at least wanted to.

Larry Sheets came up with me through the minor leagues. We were both second-round picks in the 1978 draft. He was a big, strong left-handed hitter and he really dominated in rookie ball, leading the league in home runs and RBIs. But Larry was only eighteen, and he developed a case of homesickness.

After our rookie-league season, we were invited to the instructional league, where the coaches tried to make him into a catcher. Maybe all that was a little overwhelming. Whatever the case, Larry ended up quitting and went to college to play basketball.

As for me, I went on up the ladder without Larry Sheets, but eventually he came back to pro ball, and we were reunited in 1980 in Double A ball. Larry subsequently made it to the big leagues and had a really good career, and I spent plenty of time just hanging out with him, not talking about anything deep, just wiping the same mud off our jerseys or sharing a ride to the ballpark.

Have a Mentor, and Be One, Too

When you're seventeen or eighteen, one of you can't be the "dad" with the wisdom, but you can just be there, playing cards, going to a bar (though I was too young at first), living in a crummy apartment, and searching for a decent, cheap meal. It's friend-mentoring. You may not even realize you're doing it at the time, but sharing circumstances or experience makes it easier. Ask Larry Sheets. Or one of the kids in our program.

Darts—pointed lessons

One night while I was hanging out with my son Ryan, we decided to play darts. I've played a lot and I'm reasonably good. He, on the other hand, has hardly ever played, but as we talked, I caught him watching me and learning.

As we played, he told me some stuff about his experiences in the minor leagues. There was one time he blew his ankle out in the Gulf Coast League and somebody in the clubhouse said, "Your dad played seventeen years without getting hurt, and you can't get in one game without getting hurt." That's not easy to take. I could have said you have to ignore stuff like that, or confront the jerks who say it, or just play the game and show them what you're made of. Instead, I just let him talk, and eventually he shook his head, laughed a bit, and we moved on.

As our darts game continued, he began to wonder what he'll do if he doesn't make it in baseball. He's got two years of college as a business major; he's very smart, and he has an eye for the structure of the game.

There were any number of things I could have said. He could be in a front office, be a coach, or even work with me at Ripken Baseball. I could have told him to just be a player, period. Then, if it doesn't work out, that's when you figure out what to do next. He shouldn't be looking at how long he's been at it. Instead, he needs to focus on the day-to-day and then do what he can to control the things he can control. Make adjustments, learn from the adjustments, and when the day of reckoning comes, it comes.

I didn't say any of that. I just let him say whatever he was thinking and feeling out loud. The whole time, we were playing darts. And what started out as my running up a high score on him evolved to his holding his own and eventually to our having a real battle—which he won. That made me feel good. That's mentoring that works. It's almost invisible, but sometimes that's the best kind.

Chapter 8

How to Be the Quietest Person in the Room

I've always believed you learn more by listening than by talking. I didn't invent that idea, but I've noticed that very few people follow it. I realized long ago there's more that I don't know than I do know, so listening to myself is just an echo, not a new idea. The smartest people I've ever known are good listeners. And, if you listen, the other guy, even your opponent, may tell you what it takes to win.

Listen, watch, learn.

Shortstop homework

You don't get to be a major-league shortstop by running on the field and claiming the position. You don't talk your way into it. I learned to be a shortstop not by saying, "Hey that's my position," or even by just jumping in and doing it. I learned it by watching other shortstops, learning their moves, what worked, what didn't, and how I could adapt it to my size and style. Studying shortstops was my homework. It was the only way to play better than the other guy. You study, quietly, diligently, over and over and over, and then you run out on the diamond and you execute.

Minor-league experience, major-league lessons

The reality is, there is not a huge difference between the minor leagues and the big leagues. Pitchers in the minors throw just as hard as the ones in the bigs; batters all have good eyes; fielders field smart; managers strategize. The key difference is that players in the majors execute better and way more consistently. But baseball is the same game in the minor leagues as it is in the major leagues. This means that the experience you gain in the minors—every little thing—can be applied to the big-league game.

Lots of players get intimidated when they get called up to their parent club. I know I did. The stadiums are bigger and packed with fans, you're on TV every night, and now you're suddenly playing against the best players in the world. Although I was naturally a bit intimidated, I could still call up my experiences in the minors. What worked and what didn't? How could I apply the lessons in the major leagues?

The 1983 World Series was one of those times when I drew on my minor-league know-how.

I'd never played in an AL pennant game, let alone a World Series, until that year. Three years earlier, though, I had helped the Charlotte Orioles win the AA Southern League championship. That season, I had a breakout year and hit 25 home runs. True, there were no cameras on us, no commentators in the booth, no national or international audiences, but to us, at the time, it was "the championship."

I thought back to that experience when we started the World Series against the Philadelphia Phillies. With guys like Mike Schmidt, Steve Carlton, Joe Morgan, Pete Rose, and Garry Maddox on their roster, we knew they were going to be tough, but they were also getting a bit long in the tooth; in fact, they were nicknamed the Wheeze Kids. After losing game one, we won the next three. Because Philly is just up the road from Baltimore—they called it the I-95 Series—the stands at Veterans Stadium had plenty of Orioles fans in them. I wasn't hitting very well, but the team was, so I focused on my fielding. Scott McGregor pitched like a master, throwing a shutout in game five, with only five hits and two walks. Thanks to a homer by Eddie Murray, another from Rick Dempsey, then a two-run homer from Eddie that scored me after a walk, plus Al Bumbry scoring Dempsey on a sacrifice fly, we were up 5–0.

In the ninth inning, we were one out away from winning the World Series. Their last hope was Garry Maddox, who had hit the Phillies' game-winning home run in game one, and who had gotten two of the five hits against McGregor that game. Scotty McGregor got the count to 0–2 on Maddox, but he hit a hard line drive toward the hole between shortstop and third. I was there; I grabbed it for the third out, and we won. Scott McGregor had a complete game shutout, and we were the World Series champs. For me, it was just like the Southern League championship. OK, not exactly, but I had been able to bring to mind a lesson I'd learned in the minors: when one thing isn't going well, focus on what's working. I had just made the last out to win a World Series ring, but I couldn't have done it without my minor-league experience.

Silent partner—winning with dignity

Art Modell was one of the true founders of what we now recognize as professional football. He was the lifelong owner of the Cleveland Browns (a franchise that later became the Baltimore Ravens), and he was the visionary behind televising games.

In 1999, Art started exploring the idea of selling his team. He said the decision to sell was the second hardest one he'd ever made. The hardest was leaving Cleveland, which he resisted for years, in spite of the economic pressures and political issues. When it came time to find a new owner, there was no shortage of wealthy moguls eager to add an NFL franchise to their portfolio. But Art wanted someone who cared about the game, about his cherished team, someone who would be sensitive to his family and their long identity with the franchise. When Steve Bisciotti, a Baltimore entrepreneur who had built a tech-staffing business from scratch to a $16 billion enterprise, came along, he told Modell his priorities were keeping the team in his hometown, strengthening its connection to the community, building toward a championship, and learning as much as he could from the elder owner. Bisciotti didn't talk price or ask how soon he could take over. Instead, he said he'd prefer that Art Modell and his sons maintain control for at least another year after a deal had been struck. When the Ravens won the Super Bowl that year—2001—Art Modell, who by then had agreed to sell a controlling interest to Bisciotti, accepted the Lombardi Trophy flanked by his sons, and Steve Bisciotti stood quietly and anonymously in the background, watching.

After over fifty years in the NFL, Art Modell and his family had their moment.

Over the next eleven months, Bisciotti met with Modell every week, walked the field with him, met the front-office staff and the coaches and players, and saw the rapport Art had with everyone. When the team and its partner Under Armour built a new state-of the-art facility, Bisciotti had a beautiful office built for Art Modell a few feet down the hall from his own, complete with a balcony overlooking the practice field. Bisciotti even provided a personal golf cart for the former owner, who was by then unable to get around easily, so Art could continue his daily visits up and down the sidelines of the field.

By the time the Ravens reached their second Super Bowl, in 2013, Steve Bisciotti had learned a lot about owning an NFL team. When they won, he graciously accepted the Lombardi Trophy and then gave the credit to GM Ozzie Newsome, head coach John Harbaugh and his staff, and the players. Then he stepped back into the crowd to quietly go on watching and learning.

You don't have to be in school to go to school

When you're a professional athlete, you spend a lot of time traveling, a lot of time in hotel rooms, and you have a lot of downtime in between. I figured I'd take advantage of all that time and learn about things other than what I was doing every day.

In high school, besides playing sports, I was a serious student. I made the honor roll and was being courted by several colleges when I was drafted by the Orioles. But just because I didn't make it to college didn't mean I should stop learning. (LeBron James is another athlete who didn't go to college. He was in the NBA right out of high school, but he reads every spare minute he has.) I didn't want to be a one-dimensional, baseball-only guy when I got out of the game.

These days, between my business and giving talks, I travel almost as much as I did when I played, so I still use my time the same way. Now I read newspapers and books, mostly nonfiction, especially history and business. I never wanted to be a guy who knows how you turn a double-play but not a lot about the world, so I keep on "going to school." There's always something more to learn.

Listening at parties

Starting when I was a young, up-and-coming ballplayer, I'd get invited to events and parties filled with a lot of very important people. Even though some of them might like meeting a big leaguer, they themselves were *really* in the big leagues—of politics, business, entertainment, journalism, the stuff that runs the world.

Washington Post columnist George Will is sort of the flip side of me. I know baseball, but I was always out to learn whatever else I could. George studied philosophy and politics, won a Pulitzer Prize, and is a Sunday morning news show guest and author, but he loves sports and taught himself to be an expert, especially on baseball. He and his wife, Mari, would invite me to their dinner parties, and it was there that I got to meet all kinds of DC big shots—a mix of Republicans and Democrats, governors, senators, ambassadors, you name it. Most of the time I was quiet as a church mouse. At first, it was because I was a shy kid, but later it was because I realized this was a chance to learn. If I listened, I could find out what was really going on in the world. I remember meeting Supreme Court Justice Antonin Scalia. He would own the table with his conversation: smart, funny, quick, and on top of every issue. I wasn't the only one being quiet. The whole room was hanging on his every thought. Sometimes the talk would turn to sports, and then I'd weigh in a little, but honestly, I preferred listening to talking. It was an education, one that came with a great meal.

I'm not a young kid in baseball anymore, so I'm not usually intimidated, but I still listen more than I talk, especially at those kinds of events. For the past few years, I've been a guest at the Alfalfa Club's annual dinner, thrown by and for a collection of movers and shakers in Washington, DC. The night before a recent dinner, my wife, Laura, and I were invited to Fred Malek's house for a small predinner of about thirty. The guest list included the vice president, Mike Pence; CIA director Mike Pompeo, who became secretary of state; Secretary of Transportation Elaine Chao and her husband, Senate Majority Leader Mitch McConnell; former CIA director David Petraeus; former secretary of state Madeleine Albright; past speaker of the House Newt Gingrich; Speaker of the House Paul Ryan . . . I mean, wow. Once in a while somebody would ask me a baseball question, and I'd offer my thoughts, but then I went right back to listening.

Opportunities like that don't come along often, and I'm lucky to have been included, but every day there are interesting people around who have a lot to offer, *if* you listen. Keep your mouth shut and your ears open, and you can get a free education.

Don't be just a fan; be a student

When we were growing up, we sometimes got the chance to meet big-league players, either on the Orioles or on other teams. Dad was clear that we shouldn't be awestruck fans asking for autographs. Instead, we should take advantage of the opportunity to learn something. If you had a moment at a Zen master's knee, would you just ask for an autograph (or a selfie)? When I met Boog Powell, Brooks Robinson, Reggie Jackson, and Jim Palmer, I tried to think of a question to ask. How do you hold a curveball? Do you think about hitting a home run or just trying to connect? Who's the toughest pitcher you've faced? What's your two-strike approach?

I didn't always get an answer. Sometimes a guy was just worn out after a game, or he didn't have time, but often I would get an answer. I did everything I could to commit their Zen-master wisdom to memory, and I was able to use a lot of it later. I didn't have a collection of autographs, but I had something more valuable.

I followed my dad's advice when I went into business, too. When I met with the governors of Maryland and South Carolina about building ballparks, when I sat at the table with the creative geniuses at Disney about a joint project, when a visionary entrepreneur put me on the board of his digital game company, when I later met Warren Buffett, and President Clinton, and General Colin Powell, I didn't ask for autographs or selfies. I asked questions, and I took to heart the answers.

Lessons in quiet study

Jim Collins, in his book *Good to Great*, makes the distinction between being a lecturer versus a sharer of information. The lecturer might be smart and might have accomplished a lot, but there's less of a connection with the audience because he or she is just rattling off facts or advice or success stories, and it's left to the listener to figure out if or how to use the information.

Sharers, on the other hand, have a lot to offer because what they say tends to apply to what the audience actually does and needs, and they offer a plan for using the information in the future. In that case, it's not about the speaker; it's about the listener.

I ran into Jim Collins once when we both were speaking at the same event. In the spirit of learning by asking questions, I asked him what was the best piece of advice given to him? He said it was from one of his professors, and the advice was to try to be interested instead of interesting. I love that simple distinction. It's another way of saying listen rather than talk. And when I do my talks, I try to think about what my audience needs, rather than what I need.

The wise old owl

Listen to what other people are saying . . . or not saying. Silences tell a lot.

When we explore sites for a new baseball venue, we don't go in with a major presentation, full of all the answers. Instead, our slides are a collection of questions. In Ron Shapiro's negotiation seminars, he refers to that way of working as "probing." I didn't always fully understand that concept.

A few years ago, we set out to convince Bill Marriott to allow us to change the model of his hotel to a building that looked more like the warehouse at Oriole Park at Camden Yards. I really wanted this to happen and worked hard on a presentation. But I did it without taking the time to learn much about the history of the

Marriott brand. I forged ahead with why building it our way was important to *us*.

Right before the meeting with Bill and his group from Marriott, someone on their team told me that Bill was a very good listener, and that he remains amazingly quiet during meetings. Though I'd been warned, it still affected me—no matter what I said, I couldn't seem to get a reaction from him. The quieter he was, the more I felt I had to talk. The good news was, after it was all over, Bill had indeed been a good listener and had understood what we were trying to accomplish. Despite my lack of knowledge about his brand and his company's goals, he nevertheless agreed to build a Residence Inn and Courtyard in a big brick building that resembled the Camden Yards Warehouse. Still, I learned a big lesson that day about probing, about looking at problems through all eyes. It worked out that time, but I almost blew it by not understanding Marriott more fully. I would've benefited by asking questions and listening first.

My friend, colleague, lawyer, and business mentor, Robert Altman, is the hardest-working person I know, but despite all of his success, he prefers to keep a low profile. Bob says, "I want our electronic games to be famous, not me." In fact, he'll probably be a little miffed that I included him in this book.

Bob often quotes the nursery rhyme "The Wise Old Owl":

> A wise old owl sat in an oak.
> The more he heard, the less he spoke.
> The less he spoke, the more he heard.
> Why can't we all be like that wise old bird?

That wise old bird Robert Altman has provided a great model to aspire to. Again, the lesson is to listen, rather than to talk.

Quiet on the biggest day of my life

On September 6, 1995, I passed Lou Gehrig's record of 2,130 consecutive games. It was important for me to perform well and for our team to play well, so I tried to treat it as just another game. I kept reminding myself to use my eyes and ears just as in every other game, to be always alert and aware, and to let the game unfold naturally.

It was still an overwhelming night.

We were playing the California Angels, and Camden Yards was packed. I was at shortstop and had even hit a home run earlier in the game. We were up 3–1 in the fifth, and the crowd started to cheer in the top of the inning, with two outs and the Angels batting. One more out in the fifth and the game would be official, and so would the record. Damon Easley popped out to our second baseman, Manny Alexander, and the crowd stood up, it seemed all at once, all applauding, all cheering. The half inning over, I trotted to the dugout, as always, and tossed my glove down, as always. But this time, the guys on my team surrounded me, congratulating me, pounding me on the back. The clapping continued as the numbers 2,131 revealed on the Camden Yards warehouse.

I went up to the top step and waved to the crowd and to Dad and Mom up in the skybox. Mom was crying. I spotted my kids in the front row behind the screen, too. All the while, the crowd was still on its feet, still cheering. I came out for another curtain call, waved, and said thank you. I went back to the dugout only to be called out again. Finally, on about the third or fourth curtain call, I came out of the dugout and was pushed toward the right field line by Bobby Bonilla and Rafael Palmeiro.

They said I had to take a lap or the game would never resume, so I did.

It was a glorious trip around the ballpark, turning the big celebration into many smaller, intimate ones with fans and friends along the way. I even got to shake the hand of every player on the Angels team. The celebration lasted a full twenty minutes during the middle of the fifth inning. The best part? I got to take it all in without saying a word. I would find out later that almost as amazing was the fact that the ESPN announcer Chris Berman also didn't say a word for that entire twenty minutes, either. He just let it play out, just the way it was happening.

I knew that my time to talk would come after the game at the official celebration. I'd thought a lot about what I'd say. First there were gifts and mementos. Then there were emotional, powerful speeches by my friend, O's outfielder Brady Anderson, and Lou Gehrig's team-mate Joe DiMaggio. Then Orioles owner Peter Angelos spoke. He congratulated me and announced a gift the team and he were giving to Johns Hopkins Medicine in honor of the record.

Then it was time to speak. After letting my work speak for me throughout my career, through the minors and majors and 2,131 games, I finally put my feelings into words, a few carefully chosen words, which ended this way:

"I know that if Lou Gehrig is looking down on tonight's activities, he isn't concerned about someone playing one more consecutive game than he did. Instead, he's viewing tonight as just another example of what is good and right about the great American game. Whether your name is Gehrig or Ripken, DiMaggio or Robinson, or that of some youngster who picks up his bat or puts on his glove, you are challenged by the game of baseball to do your very best day in and day out. And that's all I've ever tried to do. Thank you."

Next day, I went back to work.

Epilogue

Recently, my wife, Laura, got a call from the United States Supreme Court, from the office of Chief Justice John Roberts himself. Laura is a judge, so it's not a huge leap to think another judge might call her—but Chief Justice Roberts? I quickly understood this was not an everyday event. As my wife reminded me, there are only nine justices of the Supreme Court in the United States and only one chief justice. It turned out we were being invited to a musical celebration. Justice Ruth Bader Ginsburg plans the event annually and Chief Justice Roberts has a surprise for her every year. This year, the surprise was me.

Justice Ginsburg has been an opera fan since she was eleven years old, so appropriately enough, that night two opera singers had been invited to perform. Once they were done, Justice Roberts gave his closing remarks. His theme was substitution because the singers this year were replacements for a couple of performers who couldn't make it, and in talking about what it meant to substitute for someone, Justice Roberts told the story of Wally Pipp and Lou Gehrig. By now you know who Wally Pipp was, but when Chief Justice Roberts asked the assembled crowd if anyone knew of Pipp, only a few hands where raised. He said that this was a story of substitution. But, as he pointed out, it is also a story about showing up. He told the crowd that Gehrig's record was said to be unbreakable but that unbreakable record was broken by the man who had become known as the Ironman of Baseball, Cal Ripken. He explained that the Supreme Court had an Ironwoman, who like the Ironman, showed up every day through illness and injury. Justice Ginsburg, at eighty-five, was recovering from broken ribs and still working. Justice Roberts said he thought it only appropriate that the Ironwoman of the Supreme Court meet the Ironman of Baseball. As heads turned in surprise, I walked up to very gently hug a woman who has showed up every day and like a good teammate made the other eight justices better by her presence.

That night, I got to meet Justice Roberts and Justice

Ginsburg and we talked for a while about just showing up. I couldn't help but think of my dad, all the things he'd taught me, and how proud he'd be if he could see me chatting with the greatest legal minds of my generation. It was a long way from being expected to clear the snow off the entire sidewalk, from tales of Brooks Robinson or the minor leagues, and from the first game of the streak, or the last, but in fact, it was all the same thing: we showed up. Ruth Bader Ginsburg shows up. We do our best, we hope we've done the right thing, and then the next day, we show up again, ready to hit a baseball, or make a ruling, or raise a kid, or be kind to the person serving us in a store.

We only get a few innings on this planet, after all. May as well show up, ready to play, for every one.

Acknowledgments

Thanks most of all to Cal Ripken Jr. for the opportunity to help convey his life lessons. And thanks to agents David Larabell/CAA and David Black/David Black Agency; our editor, Luke Dempsey, and his combined baseball-literary expertise; Luke's editorial assistant, Haley Swanson; Glenn Valis, Cal's scheduling maestro; and to my wife, Ellen, for everything else in life.

—James Dale

About the Authors

CAL RIPKEN JR. was a nineteen-time All-Star over his twenty-one-year career and won the World Series with his hometown Baltimore Orioles in 1983. He is perhaps best known for breaking Lou Gehrig's Iron Man consecutive game streak of 2,131 games, going on to play 2,632 straight games. Since retiring in 2003, Ripken has devoted his life to youth baseball. Ripken Baseball operates destination youth baseball facilities in Aberdeen, Maryland; Pigeon Forge, Tennessee; and Myrtle Beach, South Carolina. He is a bestselling author and speaker, visiting multiple cities each year, and a leading baseball television analyst.

JAMES DALE has collaborated on a number of books, on sports, business, medicine, and life lessons, among other topics. His works include *The Power of Nice* and *Bullies, Tyrants, and Impossible People,* both with agent-negotiator Ron Shapiro; and *Together We Were We Eleven Foot Nine* with Hall of Fame pitcher Jim Palmer.